SONG OF
SOLOMON

◆

SONG OF SOLOMON

$\blacklozenge$

H. A. IRONSIDE

Revised Edition

Introductory Notes by
John Phillips

LOIZEAUX
Neptune, New Jersey

First Edition, 1933
Revised Edition, 1999

Song of Solomon
© 1999 by Loizeaux Brothers

A Publication of Loizeaux Brothers, Inc.
*A Nonprofit Organization Devoted to the Lord's Work
and to the Spread of His Truth*

Unless otherwise indicated, Scripture quotations are taken from
the King James version of the Bible.

Profile taken from *Exploring the Scriptures*
© 1965, 1970, 1989 by John Phillips

Library of Congress Cataloging-in-Publication Data

Ironside, H. A. (Henry Allan), 1876-1951.
Song of Solomon / H. A. Ironside.—Rev. ed. / introductory
notes by John Phillips.
p. cm.
Rev. ed. of: Addresses on the Song of Solomon. 1st ed. 1933.
ISBN 0-87213-405-9 (pbk.: alk. paper)
1. Bible. O.T. Song of Solomon—Commentaries.
I. Ironside, H. A. (Henry Allan), 1876-1951.
Addresses on the Song of Solomon.
II. Title.
BS1485.3.I76   1999
223'.907—dc21   98-45395

Printed in the United States of America
10 9 8 7 6 5 4 3 2 1

CONTENTS

SONG OF SOLOMON
A BOOK OF LOVE

BY JOHN PHILLIPS

S olomon wrote 3,000 proverbs and 1,005 songs (1 Kings 4:32). He was wiser than all the fabled philosophers of his day, for his wisdom was a direct gift from God (1 Kings 3:12). He wrote three of the books of the Bible. And, although we do not know for sure the order in which they were written, presumably he wrote the Song of Solomon when he was young and in love, Proverbs when he was middle-aged and his intellectual powers were at their zenith, and Ecclesiastes when he was old, disappointed, and disillusioned with the carnality of much of his life.

Picture the background against which Solomon wrote his books. The wealth and wisdom of Solomon were the talk of every kingdom and tribe of his day. His great Tarshish ships plied the trade lanes of the Mediterranean and also found their way down the coastline of East Africa to Arabia and India, so that into Jerusalem flowed the exotic traffic of the East. Great caravans of camels crossed the deserts, bearing back riches for the king and spreading his fame far and wide.

From all over the East men came to hear the wisdom of Solomon. They talked with bated breath of the godlike judgment that had suggested carving up a living child to share him half and half with two women, each claiming him as her own, thus revealing the true mother. His fame reached far south to Ethiopia from whence came the queen of Sheba, all the long perilous way up the Nile, across burning sands and on up the steep hill country of Judah to sit at the feet of Solomon. Then, as at last she turned back toward home, it was with an ache in her heart and a confession on her lips: "The half was never told me."

Such was Solomon! But as the years slipped away, sad and serious were the mistakes he made, entering into political marriages with the daughters of pagan kings. Gradually his spirituality declined as his Oriental luxury and opulence increased, and his harem dinned like Babel with hundreds of strange tongues. Jerusalem became the home of heathendom also, as Solomon's wives imported their pagan gods and erected shrines to them. As Solomon began to lose his vision of the true and living God, he began to degenerate into a common Eastern despot. He multiplied his slaves, ground onerous taxes from his subjects, and at last followed his outlandish wives into the abominable rites of Ashtoreth and worshiped the abomination of the Zidonians, and even engaged in the savage worship of Milcom and Moloch. It is against this background of wisdom and wealth, women and worship that the books of Solomon should be read.

If one book of the Bible may be said to be more sacred than another, then the Song of Solomon is that book, the very holy of holies of Scripture. The man with an impure mind will never understand this book. Under the figure of a bride and a bridegroom is expressed the love of Christ for His own, and the love that each believer has for his Lord. There is no sin, therefore, no shame.

There are several important interpretations for this book. The two main positions usually taken differ in their identification of the bridegroom of the Song.

According to one interpretation the bridegroom is Solomon, and the bride, a certain Shulamite woman. The Shulamite is seen awaiting the arrival of Solomon and, surrounded by ladies of the court, pouring out her rapture and longing. The king appears and takes her to his banqueting house, where the two lovers commune together. Then the Shulamite again confides in the court ladies, telling what tender regard she has for her beloved. With an overflowing heart she sings of the way in which her beloved king found her and wooed her; of how all nature awoke to new loveliness; of how she lost him, found him again, and would not let him go. After this, Solomon is seen approaching Jerusalem with his bodyguard, wearing a splendid crown. He addresses the Shulamite with words of love, and to these she responds briefly but with rapturous delight. Then a cloud passes over the scene. Under the figure of a dream the bride describes a temporary separation of heart from her groom, her misery, her longing and search for him, and her appeal to her court companions to help her. In response to their questions the Shulamite tells why she loves her beloved so. Solomon returns and once more the two are united amid words of praise and assurances of love. The bride invites her husband to return with her to the scenes of her maiden life, and they are next seen enjoying the simplicity of country life, exchanging remembrances and confidences. Others are thought of, and the bride's joy reaches out to her kindred. The Song ends with the bride singing and bidding her beloved to hasten to her side. In this view of the Song, Solomon is taken to be a type of Christ and the Shulamite a type of the church.

Another view of the Song sees three main speakers and several subsidiary speakers. Solomon is seen as representing the world; the Shulamite, the church; and the Shulamite's shepherd-fiancé, Christ. Solomon used all the dazzle and splendor of his court to woo the girl away from her true love, seeking to get her to become one of his wives instead. In like manner the world is ever seeking to attract away from Christ those who are "espoused" to Him. Solomon is unable to accomplish his goal, however, for the Shulamite resists all his overtures and remains true to her beloved shepherd to whom, at last, she is reunited.

The abiding value of the Song of Solomon is clear whichever view is taken. As human life finds its highest fulfillment in the love of man and woman, so spiritual life finds its highest fulfillment in the love of Christ and His church.

PREFACE

TO THE REVISED EDITION

In revising Dr. Ironside's *Addresses on the Song of Solomon* we have divided the text into chapters corresponding to those found in this book of the Old Testament. We hope this division will make it more compatible with methods used by today's Bible student. No material was omitted, although it may seem to the reader that such is the case, especially in regard to the brevity of chapters 6 and 7. As Dr. Ironside wrote in the preface to the 1933 edition:

> The little volume now before the reader consists of revised notes, considerably abbreviated, of addresses delivered in the Moody Memorial Church, Chicago....The attentive reader will realize at once that there has been no attempt to fully expound the Song, but rather to stress in each address some one or more of the outstanding features of the particular portion discussed....If God be pleased to own this attempt to create a greater yearning for fellowship with Himself and to lead the way into a deeper knowledge of the love of Christ, the labor expended will be well worth while.

The Publisher

INTRODUCTION

The Song of Solomon is a little book that has held a peculiar attraction for many of the people of God all through the centuries. Yet others have had great difficulty in understanding just why such a book should have a place in the canon of Holy Scripture at all. Frequently I have heard those who should have known better say that they could see nothing of spiritual value in this little book; they questioned very much whether it was really entitled to be considered as part of the inspired Word of God. As far as that is concerned, it is not left to the church in our day to decide which books should belong to the canon of Scripture and which should be omitted. Our blessed Lord Jesus Christ has settled that for us, at least as far as the Old Testament is concerned. When He was here on earth He had exactly the same Old Testament that we have. It consisted of the same books, no more and no less.

Those that are sometimes called the Apocryphal books did not belong to the Hebrew Old Testament, which Christ valued, fed on, and commended to His disciples. He placed His divine imprimatur on the Scriptures when He referred to the entire volume and said, "the scripture cannot be broken" (John 10:35). Therefore we do not have to raise any question as to the inspiration of the Canticles. He declared the Hebrew Bible to be the Word of the living God.

There are many figures from this little book in various parts of the New Testament, for instance, the well of living water (John 4); the veiled woman (1 Corinthians 11); the precious fruit (James 5:7); the spotless bride (Ephesians 5:27); unquenchable love (1 Corinthians 13:8); love strong as death (John 15:13); ointment poured forth (John 12:3); draw me (John 6:44); the Shepherd leading His flock (John 10:4,5,27); and the fruits of righteousness (Philippians 1:11). Who can fail to see allusions to the Song of Solomon in all these figures?

If we grant that it is inspired, what then are its lessons? Why do we have it in Holy Scripture? Many of the Jewish teachers thought of it simply as designed by God to give a right understanding of conjugal love. They thought of it as the glorification of the bliss of wedded life. If we conceived of it from no higher standpoint than this, it would mean that it had a right to a place in the canon. Wedded life in Israel represented the very highest, fullest, and deepest affection at a time when, in the nations surrounding Israel, woman was looked on as mere chattel. She was considered a slave or the object of man's pleasure to be discarded when and as he pleased. But it was otherwise in Israel. The Jewish home was a place where love and tenderness reigned; no doubt this little book had a great deal to do with lifting it to that glorious height.

But down through the centuries, the more spiritually minded in Israel saw a deeper meaning in this Song of Solomon; they recognized the design of God to illustrate the mutual love subsisting between Jehovah and Israel. Again and again in other Scriptures, Jehovah is likened to a bridegroom and Israel to His chosen bride; so the spiritually minded Israelites in the years before Christ, came to look at the Song in this way. They called it "the Book of Communion." It is the book that sets forth Jehovah and His people in blessed and happy communion.

All through the Christian centuries those who have had an insight into spiritual truth have thought of it from two standpoints. First, as typifying the wondrous relationship that subsists between Christ and the church. It is the glowing heart, the enraptured spirit of our blessed Lord revealing Himself to His redeemed people as her Bridegroom and her Head, and the church's glad response. And second, from a moral standpoint, it illustrates the relationship between an individual soul and Christ. How many a devoted saint has exclaimed with gladness, "I am my beloved's, and his desire is toward me" (7:10).

Rutherford's meditations were evidently based on this little book when he exclaimed:

Oh, I am my Beloved's,
And my Beloved's mine;
He brings a poor vile sinner
Into His house of wine;
I stand upon His merit,
I know no safer stand,
Not e'en where glory dwelleth
In Immanuel's land.

Therefore we may think of the book from four standpoints. Looking at it literally, we see the glorification of wedded love. Looking at it from a dispensational standpoint, we see the relationship between Jehovah and Israel. Redemptively, we find the wonderful relationship between Christ and the church. And studying it from the moral or spiritual standpoint, we see it as the book of communion between an individual soul and the blessed, glorified, risen Lord.

It is a bit difficult to get the exact connection of the different portions of the book. It is not a drama, as the book of Job is; it does not present to our consideration any continuous story. It consists rather of a series of love lyrics, each one complete in itself. It is the lover with enraptured heart setting to music the thrill of the soul. Thus you have this cluster of song-flowers, each one setting forth some different phase of communion between the beloved and the one so loved. And yet, behind it all, there must be some kind of story. What is this background?

Around a hundred years ago, Ewald, the great German critic who has been called the father of higher criticism, suggested that the story was something like this. In the hill country north of Jerusalem there was a family in charge of a vineyard belonging to King Solomon. The young daughter of the family, a shepherdess, had been won by a shepherd who had drawn her heart to himself, and their troth had been pledged. But as King Solomon rode along the lane one day he saw this young shepherdess in the vineyard, and his heart went out to her. He determined to win her for himself and so tried by blandishment to stir up her affections. But she was true to her sylvan admirer. Eventually the king actually had her kidnapped and taken to his palace to the royal harem. There again and again he pressed his suit and tried to alienate her from her shepherd lover in the hills. Sometimes she was almost tempted to yield, for her case seemed a hopeless one; but then she would remember her former lover, and she would say, "No, I cannot turn from him. I am my beloved's, and his desire is toward me." Finally King Solomon set her free and she went back to the one she loved.

That background story of the Song of Solomon has been accepted by a great many Bible students. I have been a little surprised at times to hear some of my fundamental brethren advocating this viewpoint apparently without realizing its source. Personally, I reject it. I do not think it at all likely that a man like Ewald, who had no real spiritual insight, ever understood this little book of communion. This man started the present modern trend of refusing to recognize the true inspiration of the Bible. It does not seem to me that the Spirit of God would use such a man to open up this little book to us.

There are several other reasons why I refuse this view. First and foremost, it makes King Solomon the villain of the story. When we turn to the Word of God, we find that Solomon is viewed by the Holy Spirit of God as a type of the Lord Jesus Christ. In the Psalms Solomon is portrayed as the prince of peace succeeding David after years of warfare and picturing Christ's coming again to reign as Prince of peace. In the New Testament we read the words of the Lord Jesus, "The queen of the south shall rise up in the judgment with this generation, and shall condemn it: for she came from the uttermost parts of the earth to hear the wisdom of Solomon; and, behold, a greater than Solomon is here" (Matthew 12:42). When I say that Solomon is a type of Christ, I do not mean Solomon personally represented Christ. Whenever any man is spoken of as a type of Christ, you are not to think of what the man is in himself, but what he is officially. David officially was a type of Christ; David personally was guilty of very grievous sin, but the Lord is the sinless One. Solomon was guilty of very serious departure from God during certain periods of his life, but officially he represented our Lord Jesus Christ as the Prince of peace. It is not the way of the Spirit of God to present a character or object as a type of Christ in one place and a type of that which is wicked and unholy in another. And if we were to take Ewald's suggestion as the real story behind this book, we would have to think of Solomon as the type of the world, the flesh, and the devil, trying to win the heart of this young woman away from the shepherd who represents the Lord Jesus Christ.

Another reason why I reject Ewald's view is that it would mean that we would have to understand some of the most lovely and tender passages of this little book in which the king addressed himself to the shepherdess, as mere blandishment instead of a sincere and holy love. These very passages have thrilled the heart of God's people all down through the centuries. They have reveled in them, delighted in them, and fed their souls on them. It is not likely that they have been misled or that the Holy Spirit who came to guide into all truth has thus deceived, or allowed to be deceived, so many of God's most spiritual people throughout the centuries. Therefore, I refuse to take the story that I have given you from Ewald as the explanation of the Song of Solomon.

Let me give you another story, the one that came to me one day when I was alone on my knees. I had to teach this little book and was a bit perplexed about it. I did not like the story of Ewald, and so I went to the One who wrote the book and asked Him to tell me what was behind it. "Oh," you say, "did you know the Author of the book?" Yes, I have known Him for a long time. At that time I had known Him about thirty years. "Well," you say, "the book is rather a recent thing if you know the author." No, not at all, it is a very old book, but the Author is the Ancient of Days and I have known Him ever since in grace He saved my soul. And so I took Him at His word and reminded Him of His promise that when the Holy Spirit came, He would take of the things of Christ and make them clear to us. I said, "Blessed Lord, I am all perplexed about this little book; by Thy Spirit show it to me so that I will really understand its meaning." I am going to give you the story that it seemed He gave to me.

This is what I thought I could see behind the Song of Solomon. Up there in the north country, in the mountain district of Ephraim, King Solomon had a vineyard (8:11); he let it out to keepers, to an Ephraimite family. Apparently the husband and father was dead, but there was a mother and at least two sons. We read in the King

James version, "My mother's children were angry with me" (1:6). In Hebrew it is, "My mother's sons." There may have been more sons, but there were at least two. And then there were two daughters—a little one spoken of in chapter 8, "We have a little sister," and an older daughter, the Shulamite. It would seem as though this latter one was the "ugly duckling" or the "Cinderella" of the family. Her brothers did not appreciate her and foisted hard tasks on her, denying her the privileges that a growing girl might have expected in a Hebrew home. "My mother's sons were angry with me." That makes me wonder whether they were not her half brothers; if this were not a divided family.

"My mother's [sons] were angry with me; they made me the keeper of the vineyards; but mine own vineyard have I not kept" (1:6). They said to her, "No; you can't loll around the house; you get out and get to work. Look after the vineyard." She was responsible to prune the vines and to set the traps for the little foxes that spoiled the vines. They also committed to her care the lambs and the kids of the flock. It was her responsibility to protect and find suitable pasture for them. She worked hard and was in the sun from early until late. "Mine own vineyard have I not kept." She meant, "While working so hard in the field, I have no opportunity to look after myself." What girl is there that does not value a few hours in front of the mirror, the opportunity to fix her hair and to make herself attractive? She had no opportunity to care for her own person. I do not suppose she ever knew the use of cosmetics of any kind, yet as she looked out on the road she would see the beautiful ladies of the court riding on their palfreys and in their palanquins. As she got a glimpse of them, or as she bent over a woodland spring and saw her own reflection, she would say, "I am sunburned but comely, and if I only had the opportunity, I could be as beautiful as the rest of them." That is all involved in that expression, "Mine own vineyard have I not kept."

One day as she was caring for her flock she looked up, and to her embarrassment there stood a tall and handsome shepherd she had never seen before, gazing intently on her. She exclaimed, "Look not upon me, because I am black, because the sun hath looked upon me." And then she gives the explanation, "My mother's children were angry with me; they made me the keeper of the vineyards; but mine own vineyard have I not kept." But he answers quietly without any offensive forwardness, "I was not thinking of you as swarthy and sunburned and unpleasant to look upon. To my mind you are altogether lovely; behold, thou art fair, my love; there is no spot in thee." Of course that went a long way toward a friendship.

Little by little that friendship ripened into affection, and affection into love, and finally this shepherd had won the heart of the shepherdess. Then he went away, but before he went he said, "Some day I am coming back for you, and I am going to make you my bride." And she believed him. Probably no one else did. Her brothers did not believe him, and the people in the mountain country felt she was a poor simple country maiden who had been deceived by this strange man. She had inquired of him where he fed his flock, but he put her off with an evasive answer; yet she trusted him. He was gone a long time. Sometimes she dreamed of him and would exclaim, "The voice of my beloved," only to find that all was quiet and dark about her. But still she trusted him.

One day there was a great cloud of dust on the road and the country people ran to see what it meant. They saw a glorious cavalcade with the king's bodyguard and the king himself, and they stopped just opposite the vineyard. To the amazement of the shepherdess, the royal outriders came to her with the announcement, "The king has sent us for you." "For me?" she asked. "Yes, come." In obedience she went and when she looked into the face of the king, behold he was the shepherd who had won her heart. She said, "I am my beloved's, and his desire is toward me."

One great reason why I think this is the story of the Canticles is because all the way through the Holy Scriptures, from Genesis to Revelation, we have the story of the Shepherd who came from Heaven's highest glory down into this dark world that He might woo and win a bride for Himself. Then He went away, but He declared, "I will come again, and receive you unto myself." And so His church has waited long for Him to come back, but some day He is coming to fulfill His Word.

When He comes, our glorious King,
All His ransomed home to bring,
Then anew this song we'll sing:
Hallelujah, what a Savior!
                                  Philip P. Bliss

This I believe is the background of the expression of loving communion in this little book, the Song of Songs. That very title reminds you of the holy of holies; it is the transcendent song. The Jews did not allow a young man to read the book until he was thirty years of age, lest he might read into it mere sensual gratification and misuse its beautiful phrases. So we may say it is only as we grow in grace and in the knowledge of Christ that we can read this book understandingly and see in it the secret of the Lord.

SONG OF SOLOMON

CHAPTER 1

We will be glad and rejoice in thee,
we will remember thy love more than wine (4).

The first chapter divides itself into three parts. The first four verses give us the soul's satisfaction; it is the expression of the bride's delight in her bridegroom. She exclaims, "The song of songs, which is Solomon's. Let him kiss me with the kisses of his mouth: for thy love is better than wine" (1-2).

I remember a dear servant of God saying at one time, "I have sometimes wished there were only one masculine personal pronoun in the world, so that every time I say *Him* everyone would know I mean the Lord Jesus Christ." You remember Mary Magdalene saying, "They have taken away my Lord, and I know not where they have laid him" (John 20:13). Then, looking up to the one she supposed to be the gardener, she said, "Sir, if thou have borne him hence, tell me where thou hast laid him, and I will take him away" (15). She did not think it necessary to use the name *Jesus*. There was only One to her and that was the Lord who had saved her; so the enraptured soul says, "Oh, to enjoy His love, His communion; to enjoy the blessedness of finding satisfaction in Him alone."

"Because of the savour of thy good ointments thy name is as ointment poured forth, therefore do the virgins love thee" (Song of Solomon 1:3). We are reminded how the house was filled with the odor of the ointment when Mary broke her alabaster box and poured it on Jesus' head (Mark 14:3).

How sweet the name of Jesus sounds
    In a believer's ear!
It soothes his sorrows, heals his wounds,
    And drives away his fear.
                                        John Newton

Next the heart cries out, "Draw me, we will run after thee: the king hath brought me into his chambers: we will be glad and rejoice in thee, we will remember thy love more than wine: the upright love thee" (Song of Solomon 1:4). The shepherdess had been brought from the hill country into the royal palace, as you and I from the distant country into the very presence of the Lord Himself. She had been claimed by the King. What a wonderful picture we have here of real communion. How often our hearts have sung,

I am Thine, O Lord, I have heard Thy voice,
    And it told Thy love to me;
But I long to rise in the arms of faith,
    And be closer drawn to Thee.

Draw me nearer, nearer, nearer, blessed Lord,
    To the cross where Thou hast died;
Draw me nearer, nearer, nearer, blessed Lord,
    To Thy precious bleeding side.
                                        Fanny J. Crosby

No one can experience true communion with Christ until He Himself has become the all-absorbing passion of the soul. His love transcends every earthly joy, of which wine is the symbol in Scripture because of its exhilarating character. Wine portrays anything of earth that stimulates or cheers. When a worldling is sad and depressed, he says, "Give strong drink unto him that is ready to perish, and wine unto those that be of heavy hearts. Let him drink, and forget his poverty, and remember his misery no more" (Proverbs 31:6-7). And so wine speaks of the joys of earth to which we once turned before we knew Christ. But after we know Him, we say, "We will remember thy love more than wine."

I am always grieved in spirit when a young Christian comes to me with the old question, Do you think there is any harm in this or that?—any harm in the theater, in dancing, in a game of cards, in the social party that has no place for Christ? I say to myself, *If that young Christian really knew Christ, he would never ask such questions.* One minute spent in fellowship with Him is worth all the joys of earth. That is what the Song of Songs is designed to teach us.

There is a fullness in His love, a sweetness found in fellowship with Christ, of which worldly people know nothing. If you are in Christ, earthly pleasures fall off like withered autumn leaves. I often hear people singing:

> Oh, how I love Jesus,
> Oh, how I love Jesus,
> Oh, how I love Jesus,
> Because He first loved me!
> Frederick Whitfield

And yet the same people who sing this song often don't spend even half-an-hour a day over the Bible; never spend ten minutes alone with God in prayer; have very little interest in the coming together of the Lord's people to wait on Him. Invite them to a prayer meeting and they are never there, but invite them to a social evening and they are all present. It is evident that the love of Christ is not yet the controlling passion of the heart. The surrendered soul exclaims, "We will remember thy love more than wine." And in Ephesians 5:18 we read, "Be not drunk with wine, wherein is excess; but be filled with the Spirit." The Spirit-filled believer never craves the follies of the godless world. Christ is enough to satisfy at all times.

The second section of Song of Solomon 1 takes in verses 5-11 and refers to that little retrospect that I have already mentioned in the introduction to this volume. It looks back to the time when the shepherdess first met her lover and inquired of him as to where he fed his flock. He answered, "If thou know not, O thou fairest among women, go thy way forth by the footsteps of the flock, and feed thy kids beside the shepherds' tents" (1:8). In other words, it is as when the disciples of John came to Jesus and said, "Master, where dwellest thou?" And He said, "Come and see" (John 1:38-39). And so the soul cries out, "O Thou shepherd of my heart, where feedest Thou?" And He answers, "Just go along in the shepherds' path, feed your flock with the rest, and you will find out." If you take the path of devotedness to Christ, you will soon know where He dwells. If you walk in obedience to His Word you cannot fail to find Him.

The third section of chapter 1 includes verses 12-17 and presents to us a wonderful picture of communion with the king. There he and his beautiful bride are together in the royal palace, and she says, "While the king sitteth at his table [the place of communion] my spikenard sendeth forth the smell thereof. A bundle of myrrh is my wellbeloved unto me" (1:12-13). In other words, "He is to me like a fragrant nosegay in which my senses delight." And so as we enter into communion with Christ, He becomes all in all to us and the heart goes out in worship and praise, like Mary, as already mentioned, in the house of Bethany bringing her alabaster box of ointment and pouring it on the head of Jesus. The King sat at the table that day, and her spikenard emitted its fragrance and the house was filled with the odor of the ointment. There can be no real worship unless the heart is occupied with Him.

It is common nowadays to substitute service for worship and to be more taken up with hearing sermons or with ritual observances than with adoration and praise. God has said, "Whoso offereth praise glorifieth me" (Psalm 50:23). He tells us He inhabits the praises of His people (Psalm 22:3). It is the satisfied heart that really worships. When the soul has been won for Christ there will be appreciation of Him for what He is; not merely thanksgiving (important as that is) for what He has so graciously bestowed on us. "Whom having not seen, ye love; in whom, though now ye see him not, yet believing, ye rejoice with joy unspeakable and full of glory" (1 Peter 1:8). This causes the spirit to go out to Him in worship and praise.

"The Father," Jesus told the Samaritan woman, "seeketh such to worship him" (John 4:23). He yearns for the adoring love of devoted hearts. May we indeed respond to His desire and ever "worship the Father in spirit and in truth."

SONG OF SOLOMON

CHAPTER 2

He brought me to the banqueting house,
and his banner over me was love (4).

The figure of the bride and the bridegroom is used very frequently in Scripture. In the Old Testament, Isaiah said, "As the bridegroom rejoiceth over the bride, so shall thy God rejoice over thee" (62:5). It is used of the church in the New Testament: "Christ also loved the church, and gave himself for it; That he might sanctify and cleanse it with the washing of water by the word" (Ephesians 5:25-26). And when the apostle Paul spoke of the divine institution of marriage he said, "For this cause shall a man leave his father and mother, and shall be joined unto his wife, and they two shall be one flesh. This is a great mystery: but I speak concerning Christ and the church" (Ephesians 5:31-32). And then writing to the Corinthian believers he said, "I have espoused you to one husband, that I may present you as a chaste virgin to Christ" (2 Corinthians 11:2). Therefore, this delightful figure of the sweet and intimate marriage relationship is used throughout Scripture to illustrate our union and communion with the eternal Lover of our souls.

I have said that the Song of Solomon is the book of communion. We have that beautifully set forth in the first seven verses of this second chapter, where we see the bride and bridegroom conversing together. We delight to speak with those whom we love. One of the wonderful things about love is that when someone has really filled the vision of your soul, you do not feel that any time spent communing with him is wasted.

In this chapter we see the lovers out in the country together. She exclaims, for it is evidently she who speaks in verse one, "I am the rose of Sharon, and the lily of the valleys." Generally we apply those words to the blessed Lord; we speak of Him as the Rose of Sharon. We sing sometimes, "He's the Lily of the Valley, the Bright and Morning Star." It is perfectly right and proper to apply all of these delightful figures to Him; for any figure that speaks of that which is beautiful and of good report can be applied to the Lord. But the wonderful thing is that He has put His own beauty on His people. And so here the bride is looking up into the face of the bridegroom saying, "I am the rose [really, the narcissus, a blood-red flower] of Sharon, and the lily of the valleys"—the lily that thrives in the hidden place, not in the town, not in the heat and bustle of the city, but out in the cool countryside, in the quiet field. Does it not speak of the soul's separation to Christ Himself?

It is when we draw apart from the things of the world, apart to Christ, that we really thrive and grow in grace and become beautiful in His sight. I am afraid that many of us do not develop spiritually as we should, because of the fact that we know so little of this heart-separation to Himself. It grieves the heart of many who seek to lead others in the ways of Christ to know the influence that the world has on these new converts. How often the question comes from dear young Christians, "Must I give up this, and must I give up that, if I am going to live a consistent Christian life?" And the things that they speak of with such apparent yearning are mere trifles compared with communion with Him. Must I give up eating sawdust in order to enjoy a good dinner? Who would talk like that? Must I give up the pleasures of the world in order that I may have communion with Christ? It is easy to let them all go if the soul is enraptured with Him. When you get to know Him better, when you learn to enjoy communion with Him, you will find yourself turning the question around. When the world says, "Won't you participate with us in this doubtful pleasure or in this unholy thing?" your answer will be, "Must I give up so much to come down to that level?

Must I give up communion with Him? Must I give up the enjoyment of His Word? Must I give up fellowship with His people in order to go in the ways of the world?" Dear young Christian, do not think of it as giving up anything to go apart with Him and enjoy His blessed fellowship. It is then the separated soul looks into His face and says, "I am like the narcissus of Sharon, and the lily of the valleys."

The bridegroom at once responds, "As the lily among thorns, so is my love among the daughters" (2). This expresses the heart-satisfaction that Christ has in His people. See the contrast between the beautiful, fragile, lovely lily and the rough, unpleasant, disagreeable thorn. The thorn illustrates those who are still under the curse, walking in the ways of the world. The lily represents His sanctified, devoted people who have turned from the world to Himself. This is His estimate of His saints.

As this little colloquy goes on—the soul speaking to Him and He responding, a beautiful holy dialogue—the bride looks up and says, "As the apple tree among the trees of the wood, so is my beloved among the sons. I sat down under his shadow with great delight, and his fruit was sweet to my taste" (3). He says to her, "You are like a lily to me in contrast to the thorns." And she says, "And you to me are like a beautiful fruit tree in contrast to the fruitless trees of the wood." Scholars have wondered just what word should be used here to translate the name of this tree. Is it the apple tree that we know or is it the citron? The citron is a tree of a beautiful, deep green shade, producing a lovely, refreshing fruit, like a cross between our grapefruit and orange. But the thought that the bride expresses is this: You are so much more to me than any other can possibly be. I have shade and rest and refreshment in your presence. "I sat down under his shadow with great delight, and his fruit was sweet to my taste."

How often the Spirit of God employs the figure of a shadow. To understand it correctly you have to think of a hot eastern climate, with the tropical sun shining down on a traveler. Suddenly he sees before him a place of refuge and exclaims as David did in the seventeenth Psalm, "Keep me as the apple of the eye, hide me under the shadow of thy wings" (8). Again in Psalm 36:7 he said, "How excellent is thy lovingkindness, O God! therefore the children of men put their trust under the shadow of thy wings." Isaiah spoke of "the shadow of a great rock in a weary land" (32:2). This figure is used very frequently in the Bible in speaking of rest and of comfort found alone in communion with Christ.

There is no drudgery here. If you are married, do you remember when you first fell in love with your life-companion? Did you find it hard to spend half an hour with him? Did you try to find an excuse for staying away from that young lady? Did you always have some other engagement so that you would not be at home when that young man called on you? No; you tried to put everything else out of the way so as to have the opportunity to became better acquainted with the person who had won your heart. So it is with the believer. The more we get to know of Christ the more we delight in His presence. So the bride says, "I sat down under his shadow with great delight, and his fruit was sweet to my taste." Her bliss was complete.

"Delight thyself also in the Lord; and he shall give thee the desires of thine heart" (Psalm 37:4). You cannot delight in Christ if you are going after the things of the world. "No man can serve two masters: for either he will hate the one, and love the other; or else he will hold to the one, and despise the other. Ye cannot serve God and mammon" (Matthew 6:24). And so you cannot enjoy Christ and the world at the same time.

Then we go a step farther in this scene of communion. "He brought me to the banqueting house, and his banner over me was love" (4). This is the place of the soul's deep enjoyment when all else is shut out. Christ's all-satisfying love fills the spirit's vision, and the entire being is taken up with Himself. This is indeed the "house of wine," the rest of love.

In verses five and six you have the soul so completely enthralled by the one who has won her heart that she does not care to think of anything else. Then in verse seven we have the bridegroom's tender answer: "I charge you, O ye daughters of Jerusalem, by the roes, and by the hinds of the field, that ye stir not up, nor awake my

love, till [she] please," not "till he please." The word is in the feminine, and the point is this: He sees such joy in His people when they
are in communion with Him that He says, "Now do not bring in
anything to spoil this until she herself please."

We have an illustration of this joyful communion in the Gospels.
Jesus had gone to the house of Mary, Martha, and Lazarus. Martha
served and was cumbered about her serving, but Mary took her place
at the feet of Jesus and listened to His words. She was in the banqueting house and His banner over her was love. He was enjoying
communion with her. But Martha said, "I have something more
important for Mary than that; it is more important that she put the
dishes on the table and get the dinner ready." But Jesus said, as it
were, "Martha, Martha, I charge you that ye stir not up, nor awake
my love till she please." In other words, "As long as she is content
to sit at My feet and commune with Me, this means more to Me
than the most enjoyable repast."

When the poor Samaritan woman came to Jesus at the well outside the city of Sychar, His disciples came and wondered if He were
not hungry. But He said, "I have meat to eat that ye know not of"
(John 4:32). It meant more to Him to have that poor sinner listen-
ing to His words, drawing near to Him, and entering into the love of
His heart, than to enjoy the food that they had gone to the city to
get. Service is a wonderful thing; it is a great privilege to labor for
so good a Master. But there is something that comes before service,
that means more to Him and should mean more to us; that something is fellowship with Himself!

A husband was bereft of his precious wife and had just a darling
daughter left to him. In those lonely days after the wife had passed
away, he found his solace and his comfort in this beautiful girl she
had left behind. Evening after evening when he came home from
work, they would have their quiet little meal together. Then after
the dishes had been put away they would go into the sitting-room
and talk or read and enjoy each other's company. One evening toward the holiday season, after doing up the dishes, the daughter
said, "Now, Father dear, you will excuse me tonight; I have something to occupy me upstairs. You can read while I go up." So he sat

alone, and the next night the same thing happened; night after night for about two weeks he sat alone each evening. On Christmas morning the girl came bounding into his room saying, "Merry Christmas, Father dear." She handed him a beautiful pair of slippers she had made for him. He looked at them, kissed her, and said, "My darling, you made these yourself?" "Yes, Father." "Is this why I have been denied your company the last two weeks?" he asked. "Yes," she said, "this is my secret." Then he said, "That is very lovely, but next time I would rather have you than anything you can make for me." Our blessed Lord wants ourselves. Our heart's affection means far more to Him than service. There will be service, of course, but service that springs out of communion. That accomplishes a great deal more than when we are too busy to enjoy fellowship with Him.

The next section of this second chapter of the Song (verses 8-13) may be called "Love's Expectation." In this section the bridegroom is absent from his bride and she is waiting for him to return. Suddenly she thinks she hears his voice, and she springs up saying, "The voice of my beloved! behold, he cometh leaping upon the mountains, skipping upon the hills" (8). You and I who know Christ's grace realize something of what this means. He has saved us and won our hearts, as this shepherd lover won the heart of this shepherdess. He has gone away, but He said, "I will come again, and receive you unto myself" (John 14:3), and when He comes, He will be the glorious King. It was the shepherd who won her heart; it was the King to whom she was wedded. And so Jesus, the Good Shepherd, has won us for Himself, but He will be the King when we sit with Him on the throne.

Does it not stir your soul to think that at any moment we may hear His voice saying, "Arise, My love, and come away"? Listen to the way she depicts it here.

My beloved spake, and said unto me, Rise up, my love, my fair one, and come away. For, lo, the winter is past, the rain is over and gone; The flowers appear on the earth; the time of the singing…is come, and the voice of the turtle [dove] is heard in our land; The fig tree putteth forth her green figs, and the vines with the tender grape give a good smell. Arise, my love, my fair one, and come away (10-13).

It will not merely be the time of the "singing of birds", as we read in the King James version, but "the time of singing." He will sing and we will sing; we will rejoice together when earth's long winter of sorrow and trial and perplexity is ended and the glorious spring will come with our blessed Lord's return. This is just a little poem in itself, a complete love-lyric in anticipation of the bridegroom's return. We do not know how soon all this may be fulfilled for us, how soon He may come for whom our hearts are yearning. We have waited for Him through the years; we have known the cold winters, the hard and difficult days; we have known the trying times, but oh, the joy, the gladness when He comes back! He has said, "A little while, and he that shall come will come, and will not tarry" (Hebrews 10:37).

> A little while—our Lord shall come,
> And we shall wander here no more;
> He'll take us to our Father's home,
> Where He for us has gone before,
> To dwell with Him, to see His face,
> And sing the glories of His grace.
> J. G. Deck

Then we will share the glory that He went to prepare. What delight that will mean for us and for Him! He will have the joy of His heart when He has us with Him.

The closing verses speak of that which should be going on during all the time of His absence. In the first place, we ought to be enjoying Him with anticipation. Then there should be self-judgment—putting out of the life anything that would grieve or dishonor Him. The bridegroom speaks; may He speak to our souls: "O my dove, that art in the clefts of the rock" (14). That is where we are resting, in the cleft of the rock. "Rock of Ages, cleft for me, / Let me hide myself in Thee."

"O my dove, that art in the clefts of the rock, in the secret places of the stairs," or "in the hidden places of the going up." We are moving upward from day to day, soon to be with Jesus. "Let me see thy countenance, let me hear thy voice; for sweet is thy voice, and thy countenance is comely" (14). Have you heard Him saying that to you, and have you sometimes turned coldly away?

Probably when you arose in the morning you heard Him say, "Let Me see your countenance before you begin the work of the day; spend a little time with Me. Let Me hear your voice; talk with Me before you go out to speak to other people. Let Me enjoy a little time with you, the one for whom I died, before you take up the affairs of the day." And you have just turned coldly away, looked at your watch, and said, "I am sorry, but I cannot spare any time this morning; I must hasten to the office or the shop." So all day He waited for you. When evening came, He spoke again and said, "Let Me see your countenance, let Me hear your voice," and you said, "Oh, I am so tired and weary tonight, I have to hurry off to bed." Have there not been many days like that? Are there going to be many more? Or will you seek by grace to respond to the love of His heart and let Him see your face and hear your voice a little more often?

Then we have the bride's response, "Take us the foxes, the little foxes, that spoil the vines: for our vines have tender grapes" (15). You see, her brothers had driven her out to be the vinedresser. Now she thinks of that and sees a lesson there; she says in effect, "I know how I had to watch the vines so carefully, and now I have to watch the growth of my own spiritual life. As I set traps for the little foxes, so now I have to judge in myself anything that would hinder my fellowship with Him or my spiritual growth." What are the little foxes that spoil the vine? I can tell you a good many. There are the little foxes of vanity, of pride, of envy, of evil speaking, of impurity (I think this though is a wolf instead of a little fox). Then there are the little foxes of carelessness, of neglect of the Bible, of neglect of prayer, of neglect of fellowship with the people of God. These are the things that spoil the vine, that hinder spiritual growth. Deal with them in the light of the cross of Christ; put them to death before they ruin your Christian experience and do not give them any place. "Take us the foxes, the little foxes, that spoil the vines."

And now we have the closing words, "My beloved is mine, and I am his: he feedeth among the lilies" (16). We need to be reminded of this again and again. The most intimate, sweet, and unsullied spiritual relationship is brought before us here. And this is to continue, "Until the day break, and the shadows flee away" (17). When will that be? When our blessed Lord returns. "Turn, my beloved, and be thou like a roe or a young hart upon the mountains of Bether" (17), that is, the mountains of separation. He is the object of her soul as she abides on the mountains of separation until he comes back.

Oh, that these things were more real with us all! We profess to "hold" the truth of our Lord's near return. But does it hold us in such a way that we esteem all earthly things but loss for Him who is so soon to claim us wholly for Himself? "Let us search and try our ways," and make sure that we allow nothing in our lives that destroys the power of this blessed hope over our souls.

SONG OF SOLOMON

CHAPTER 3

I sought him whom my soul loveth;
I sought him, but I found him not (1).

The third chapter of this exquisite book is divided into two parts; the first comprises verses 1-5, and the second verses 6-11. The opening section sets before us interrupted and renewed communion.

We are not told just what it was that had disturbed the fellowship of the lovers. It may have been the absence of the beloved, resulting in a temporary lethargic condition on the part of his espoused one. Possibly the entire section is to be treated as a dream. In fact, this seems the most likely explanation as the opening words of chapter 3 indicate. But dreams often reflect the disturbed state of the heart. "A dream cometh through the multitude of business" (Ecclesiastes 5:3).

The opening verse depicts the restlessness of one who has lost the sense of the Lord's presence. What saint has not known such experiences? David once exclaimed, "Lord, by thy favour thou hast made my mountain to stand strong: thou didst hide thy face, and I was troubled" (Psalm 30:7). This withdrawal of the light of God's countenance is not necessarily in anger. Sometimes it is admonitory. It is love's way of bringing the soul to a realization that something is being cherished or allowed that grieves the Holy Spirit of God. Or God may withdraw His face that faith may be tested, to see whether one can trust in the dark as well as in the light. Rutherford's experience is depicted thus:

But flowers need night's cool sweetness,
The moonlight and the dew;
So Christ from one who loved Him,
His presence oft withdrew.

When Christ announced His going away to His disciples, He said, "Ye believe in God, believe also in me" (John 14:1). That is to say, "As you have believed in God whom you have never seen, so when I am absent believe in Me. I will be just as real—and just as true although to sight unseen." For though the soul may lose the sense of His presence, nevertheless He still remains faithful. He never forsakes His people though He seems to have withdrawn and He does not show Himself. This is indeed a test of faith and of true-hearted devotion. We say, "Absence makes the heart grow fonder," but there is often greater truth in the old proverb, "Out of sight, out of mind." When the Lord as a boy stayed in the temple, even Mary and Joseph went on "supposing him to have been in the company" (Luke 2:44); they did not realize the true state of affairs.

In this chapter of the Song the bride feels her loss. She seeks for him, but he is not there. There is no response to her cry. For her, rest is impossible with this awful sense of loneliness. She must seek until she finds; she cannot be contented without him. Would that this were always true of us! But sadly, how often we go on without the assurance of His presence, yet we are so insensitive that we scarcely realize our loss. The bride, however, demonstrates energy—determination—action! She must find him who is all in all to her. Love abhors a vacuum. Only the sense of his presence can fill and satisfy her heart.

In her dream—or possibly in reality—she leaves her mountain home and goes out in search of the object of her deep affections. She wends her way to the city and wanders about its streets and peers into every hidden place looking only for him! But at first her search is unrewarded. In fact it is not until she tells others of her love for him that he gladdens her vision. Note the terms used: "I sought him, but I found him not. I will seek him,...but I found him not" (1-2).

The watchmen, guarding the city at night, are surprised to see a lovely and apparently respectable woman going about at such an hour. But she turns eagerly to them before they can reprove her. She cries in the distress of her soul, "Saw ye him whom my soul loveth?" (3) The abrupt question conveyed little information indeed. To the prosaic guardians of the peace, it must have sounded almost incoherent. But to her it was all that was necessary. There was only one for whom her soul yearned. Surely they too would know his worth! But she gets no response from them.

She leaves the guards and has scarcely gone from their sight when she comes upon the object of her search. In an ecstasy of rapture she lays hold of him and clings to him as to one who might again vanish away. She brings him into her own home where she first saw the light of day.

The more the passage is pondered, the more evident it seems to be that all this happened in a dream. But it tells of the deep anguish of her soul. She missed him; she could not be happy without the sense of his presence. Her only joy was found in abiding in his love. She found him when she looked for him with all her heart.

Her attitude gratifies him. And so again we have the refrain of satisfied love. "I charge you, O ye daughters of Jerusalem, by the roes, and by the hinds of the field, that ye stir not up, nor awake my love, till [she] please" (5). As previously mentioned, the expression here is in the feminine in the original. Nothing gives our Lord more delight than to find a heart that joys in Him for what He is in Himself. Too often we think rather of His gifts, the gracious favors He bestows. It is right and proper that these should stir us to thanksgiving; but it is as we get to know Him and to joy in His love that we really worship in blissful communion.

> The bride eyes not her garment,
>   But her dear Bridegroom's face;
> I will not gaze at glory,
>   But on my King of Grace—
> Not at the crown He giveth,
>   But on His pierced hand:

The Lamb is all the glory
Of Immanuel's land.
Anne R. Cousin

The latter part of the chapter is of an entirely different character. It illustrates the truth of union rather than of restored communion. It is a little gem, complete in itself. The espoused one has waited long for the return of the shepherd whose love she has prized above all else. His promise to return for her has been cherished and relied on, even though at times his continued absence has made her heart sick with yearning and her spirit droop with fear. But never has she really lost confidence in his pledged word. Eagerly she has awaited the fulfillment of his promise.

One day all the simple folk of the countryside are astir. They are filled with interest and wonder as they behold a grand procession wending its way along the highway up from the glorious city of God. Outriders and trumpeters on prancing chargers herald the approach of a royal equipage. "Who is this that cometh?" (6) This is the question raised by every onlooker. Whose procession is this? Who travels in such grandeur and splendor? One can imagine the scene. No one can blame the curious conjectures as the peasants of the hills gaze with wonder on the advancing cavalcade. In the Hebrew the question is really, "Who is she that cometh?" It is a bridal procession. But who is the honored maiden called to share the love of the King? Evidently at first they look in vain for a sight of her. Everything proclaims a nuptial parade, but no bride is really seen.

The bridegroom, however, is clearly in evidence. It is the son of David himself. In excited admiration the wondering people exclaim: "Behold his bed, which is Solomon's" (7)! The royal conveyance is recognized. Sixty valiant soldiers guard their king as he journeys through the country. They are dressed in armor, each with his sword ready to defend his sovereign against any lurking traitorous foes. They move on in orderly array as the excitement among the shepherds and vinedressers grows ever more intense. Not often have their eyes been regaled by such a scene as this! Perhaps they will never see its like again!

How magnificent, how costly is that royal carriage! It is the King's provision for the comfort of his bride. And that bride is half-hidden among the rest of the country folk, not daring to believe that such honor is for her. All eyes are on the King. It is his crowning day—his nuptial hour—the day of the gladness of his heart. He has come forth to seek and claim his spouse whom he won as the shepherd, and to whom he now reveals himself as the King.

There is no actual mention of the claiming of the bride and bringing her to the King. But it is clearly implied. He has come to fulfill his promise to make her his own. With deep and chastened joy she responds to the royal summons and takes her place at his side. So the procession sweeps on, leaving the bewildered onlookers gasping with startled amazement at the sudden change in the situation of her who had been through the years but one of themselves. It is a worthy theme for a Song of Songs! And most graphically it portrays the glorious reality which the bride of the Lamb will soon know when the Shepherd-King comes to claim His own.

> He is coming as the Bridegroom,
>   Coming to unfold at last
> The great secret of His purpose,
>   Mystery of ages past;
> And the Bride, to her is granted,
>   In His beauty there to shine,
> As in rapture she exclaimeth,
>   "I am His, and He is mine!"
> Oh, what joy that marriage union,
>   Mystery of love divine;
> Sweet to sing in all its fulness,
>   "I am His, and He is mine!"

How short then will seem the waiting time; how trifling the follies of earth that we gave up in order to be pleasing in His sight! How slight too will the sufferings of the present time appear, as compared with the glory then to be enjoyed.

Do you think we have drawn too much on imagination as we

have sought to picture the real background of these lovely lyrics? Let me ask, Is it possible to mistake the picture when all Scripture tells the same story? What was the marriage of Adam and Eve intended to signify? What can be said of the servant seeking a bride for Isaac, and what of the love of Jacob as he served so untiringly for Rachel? What "great mystery" does Asenath, the Gentile wife of Joseph, illustrate? And what can be said of the love of Boaz for Ruth? Hosea who bought his bride in the slave market gives a darker side of the picture, yet all is in wonderful harmony. All alike tell the story that "Christ also loved the church, and gave himself for it; That he might sanctify and cleanse it with the washing of water by the word, That he might present it to himself a glorious church, not having spot, or wrinkle, or any such thing" (Ephesians 5:25-27). Then she will be "all fair" in His eyes and one with Him forever. It is written, "For this cause shall a man leave his father and mother, and shall be joined unto his wife, and they two shall be one flesh. This is a great mystery: but I speak concerning Christ and the church" (Ephesians 5:31-32).

Surely all this should speak loudly to our hearts, we who through grace have been won for One we have never yet seen. Yet we read of Him, "Whom having not seen, ye love; in whom, though now ye see him not, yet believing, ye rejoice with joy unspeakable and full of glory" (1 Peter 1:8). What will it be when we behold Him coming in royal array to claim us as His very own, when we discern in the King of kings, the Good Shepherd who gave His life for the sheep, and who, before He left this world, gave the solemn promise, "If I go...I will come again, and receive you unto myself" (John 14:3). That glad nuptial hour draws on swiftly. Well may our hearts be stirred and our spiritual pulses quickened as we join the wondering cry, "Who is this that cometh?"

When the bride is caught away, what will the astonishment be on the part of those who had never understood that she was the loved one of the Lord Most High? When they realize that the church is gone and the heavenly procession has passed them by, what will be their thoughts in that day?

But we must pause here for the present. The next chapter gives us the glad recognition and the happy response.

SONG OF SOLOMON

CHAPTER 4

Thou art all fair, my love;
there is no spot in thee (7).

It is not strange that as we think of our Lord Jesus Christ, the heavenly Bridegroom, our souls are moved to their deepest depths. But it is hard for us to realize that He has a greater love for us than we could ever possibly have for Him. And so here in this fourth chapter of the Song of Solomon, we hear the bridegroom expressing to his loved one the feelings of his heart toward her. As we read these words, as we listen to these heart-breathings, we should remember that the speaker is really our Lord Jesus Christ. The bride may be looked at in various ways, as we have already seen. Prophetically, we may think of the bride as Israel and Jehovah rejoicing over her in that coming day; individually, we may think of the bride as representing any saved soul and the Lord expressing His delight in the one He has redeemed to Himself by His precious blood; or we may view the bride as that church which Christ loved and for which He gave Himself.

So we may see in these utterances Christ's delight in His church. In verses 1-7 of this fourth chapter, you will notice that He addressed Himself directly to the bride. He spoke of her beauties as He sees them in a very wonderful way. The imagery, of course, as throughout this book, is strictly oriental. It goes considerably beyond the more commonplace language of Western culture. And yet as we read it, we see that there is nothing coarse, nothing that would cause a modest person to blush. It is the fullest, most rapturous delight of the bridegroom in the bride, but every expression is in keeping with the holiness of this blessed little book.

First, he spoke of her general appearance. Four times over in this chapter, he told her of her fairness. Twice he declared it in verse one. He said, "Behold, thou art fair, my love; behold, thou art fair." In verse seven we read, "Thou art all fair, my love; there is no spot in thee." Again in verse ten, "How fair is thy love, my sister, my spouse! how much better is thy love than wine!" And yet she had no fairness in herself, as we had no beauty in ourselves. In an earlier chapter (1:6) the bride said, "Look not upon me, because I am black, because the sun hath looked upon me." But as the bridegroom looked at her through love's eyes, he saw beauty.

Does this not bring before us the wondrous thing that our Savior has done for every one who has been redeemed by the precious blood of Christ? We would never have been saved at all if we had not realized in some measure our own wretchedness, our own sinfulness, our unlovely character. It was because of this that we fled to Him for refuge and confessed that we were anything but fair, anything but beautiful. We took our places side by side with Job and cried, "I have heard of thee by the hearing of the ear: but now mine eye seeth thee. Wherefore I abhor myself, and repent in dust and ashes" (Job 42:5-6). We knelt beside Isaiah and exclaimed, "I am a man of unclean lips, and I dwell in the midst of a people of unclean lips" (Isaiah 6:5). We took part with Peter and cried, "Depart from me; for I am a sinful man, O Lord" (Luke 5:8). But when we took that place of repentance, of acknowledgment of our own natural deformity and unloveliness, He looked upon us in His grace and said, "Thou art 'perfect [in Mine eyes] through my comeliness, which I had put upon thee'" (Ezekiel 16:14). And now as those who have been washed from our sins in His own precious blood, He addresses us in the rapturous way that we have in the Song, "Thou art all fair, my love; there is no spot in thee." What? No spot in us, when we were stained by sin, when we were polluted by iniquity? Once it could be said of us, "From the sole of the foot even unto the head there is no soundness in it; but wounds, and bruises, and putrifying sores: they have not been closed, neither bound up, neither mollified with ointment" (Isaiah 1:6). And now His holy eyes cannot find one spot of sin, nor any sign of iniquity. Let this help us to understand what grace has accomplished on our behalf: "Amazing grace, how sweet the sound, / That saved a wretch like me!" It is only God's matchless grace that has made us so accepted in the Beloved.

Then you will notice that the bridegroom looked on his bride and spoke of her countenance in the most glowing terms, referring to seven different things. First, he spoke of her eyes and said to her, "Thou hast doves' eyes within thy locks" (1). What does that mean? The dove was a clean bird, the bird of love and sorrow, the bird offered in sacrifice on the altar; it typified our Lord Jesus as the heavenly One. He saw reflected in his bride that which speaks of himself.

We may not have stopped to realize it, but the dove is very keen of sight. In an eastern city, a poor carrier pigeon fell exhausted on one of those high buildings. Somebody working on the roof of the building caught it utterly unable to rise. They found attached to it a message that had come over three thousand miles. That little dove had seen its way all along the miles and had flown on and on until at last it had brought the message to that eastern city. When our blessed Lord says to us, "Thou art fair, my love; behold, thou art fair; thou hast doves' eyes within thy locks," it means not only that we have eyes of beauty, but eyes quick to discern the precious and wonderful things that are hidden for us in His holy Word. Do we respond to this, or do these doves' eyes sometimes take to wandering, going out after the things of a poor godless world?

He said, "Thy hair is as a flock of goats, that appear from mount Gilead" (1). He referred to the Syrian goat with its long silken hair. One can imagine the beauty of the scene—a flock of goats on the mountainside. The bridegroom said, "Your hair reminds me of that." Hair, in Scripture, is a woman's glory. That is one reason why she is not supposed to follow the styles of the world and cut away her beauty and glory. You remember the woman who loved Jesus and knelt at His feet and washed them with her tears and wiped them with her hair. She was using that which spoke of her beauty and her glory to minister to Him—the loving, blessed Savior.

Yes, her hair is a woman's glory and beauty. Incidentally, that is exactly the reason why the Word of God tells the woman to cover her head when she comes into the presence of the Lord (1 Corinthians 11:5). When she comes in before Him whose glory fills the heavens, to join with His worshiping people, she is to cover her own glory that no one's attention may be distracted, but fixed on Christ Himself. When you understand these principles, you find there is a beauty and a privilege in them that does away with all legality; it also does away with the freedom to follow our own judgment. In Scripture, some things are commanded because they are right, and other things are right because they are commanded. When God makes His will known, the loyal Christian bows to His Word, assured that there is a reason for it, though he does not always understand it. How He delights to behold His obedient people; how He glories in their moral beauty!

Then, in the third place, the bridegroom speaks of the bride's teeth. We may think that strange, but there is nothing more beautiful than a lovely set of pearls half-hidden in the mouth. "Thy teeth are like a flock of sheep that are even shorn, which came up from the washing; whereof every one bear twins, and none is barren among them." The two sets of teeth correspond to the "twins" in their cleanliness and sparkling beauty, which are so attractive in his eyes. And how important the teeth are, spiritually speaking, because they speak to us of the ability to properly lay hold of and digest our food. I am afraid there are a number of toothless Christians from that standpoint. Some say, "I do not know why it is that other people read their Bibles and find such wonderful things, when I do not find much in mine." The trouble is you have such poor teeth, you do not masticate your spiritual food properly. It is by meditation that we appropriate our daily provision. David said, "My meditation of him shall be sweet" (Psalm 104:34). Until He gives you a new set of spiritual teeth, you had better use some second-hand ones. Thank God for what others have found; read their books and use them to help you in your spiritual meditation. By and by if you will wait on Him, the Lord will give you back your spiritual teeth, even if you have lost them; then you will be able to enjoy the truth for yourself.

The third verse is most lovely: "Thy lips are like a thread of scarlet, and thy speech is comely." This does not refer to the wearing of lipstick. Here it is the red lip of health, of spiritual health. "Thy speech is comely" because it is speech that has to do with Him! The bride loves to speak of the bridegroom, as the Christian loves to speak of Christ; her lips are like a thread of scarlet, for she exalts that blood by which she has been brought near to God. Every real Christian will have lips like a thread of scarlet, for he gladly confesses that he owes everything for eternity to that precious atoning blood of the Lord Jesus Christ. It is not only when we gather at the table of the Lord, when we bow in worship as we take the bread and cup as from His blessed pierced hand, that we love to sing and speak and think of the blood; but always, everywhere, at all times, the believer delights to remember that he has been redeemed to God by the precious blood of Christ. You will find the scarlet thread running right through this Song of Songs.

God has said, "The life of the flesh is in the blood: and I have given it to you upon the altar to make an atonement for your souls: for it is the blood that maketh an atonement for the soul" (Leviticus 17:11). "When I see the blood, I will pass over you" (Exodus 12:13). We have been redeemed "with the precious blood of Christ, as of a lamb without blemish...foreordained before the foundation of the world, but was manifest in these last times for you" (1 Peter 1:18-20). "The blood of Jesus Christ [God's] Son cleanseth us from all sin" (1 John 1:7). And when at last we get home to Heaven, our lips will be like a thread of scarlet still, for we will join in that new song and sing our praises to Him who was slain and has loosed us from our sins by His own blood. We will render adoration to the Lamb whose blood was shed that we might be made kings and priests unto God. O Christian, make much of the blood, speak often of the blood. Do not be satisfied with the namby-pamby, bloodless religion of the day. When you ask the question, "Are you a Christian?" and you get the ready answer, "Oh yes, I belong to the church," then see that your lips are like a thread of scarlet and ask, "Are you trusting in the precious blood of the Lord Jesus alone for salvation?" So often you will find that the idle profession made a moment ago was an empty claim made by one who is Christian in name only. There are thousands about us who know nothing of the cleansing value of the blood of Jesus.

"Thy temples are like a piece of a pomegranate within thy locks" (3). The temple speaks of the dome of thought, and so the bride's thought is about her bridegroom. She loves to think of him, to meditate on the treasures found in his words. Then he delights in her as she delights in him.

In the next verse we have the strength of her character, given her by divine grace. "Thy neck is like the tower of David builded for an armoury, whereon there hang a thousand bucklers, all shields of mighty men" (4). David's tower was the place of defense, the place of strength. The bride here is one of those who can stand up straight and boldly look the world in the face, assured of the love and protection of her matchless bridegroom. And so we are called to "be strong in the Lord, and in the power of his might" (Ephesians 6:10). The head won't be hanging down like a bulrush when our hearts are captivated by Him. We will have a boldness that is never known by those who are out of communion with Him.

Lastly, in the seventh place he spoke of that which tells of affection. "Thy two breasts are like two young roes that are twins, which feed among the lilies" (5). Her heart is his, her whole being belongs to him, and he rejoices in her. We may well sing:

> Jesus, Thou art enough
>   The mind and heart to fill;
> Thy patient life—to calm the soul;
>   Thy love—its fear dispel.
>
> O fix our earnest gaze
>   So wholly, Lord, on Thee;
> That, with Thy beauty occupied,
>   We elsewhere none may see.

As we joy in Him, we will find that He will joy in us. You remember what Faber wrote:

> That Thou should'st so delight in me
> And be the God Thou art,
> Is darkness to my intellect,
> But sunlight to my heart.

I cannot understand why He should say, "Thou art all fair, my love; there is no spot in thee" (7). I cannot comprehend such matchless grace, but my heart can rejoice in it; so I love Him in return because He first loved me.

Following this section in which we have the bridegroom's joy in the bride, in verses 8-11 we have his summons to companionship with himself. The bridegroom would call his bride away from everything else that has occupied her in order to find in him her all in all. He sees her on the mountainside. The mountain is the place of privilege, the place of beauty, of worldly grandeur and glory, but it is also the place of danger. The leopard's lair and the lion's den are there. As he beholds her there alone, he cries, "Come with me from Lebanon. . .from the lions' dens, from the mountains of the leopards." Our blessed Lord wants the companionship of His redeemed people. How sweet those words, "Come with me"! He never calls His people from anything, either the beautiful things of the world or the dangerous things (and after all, the beautiful is often the most dangerous), simply to take a path alone; it is always, "Come with Me."

You cannot afford, you who love His name, to draw back and say, "There are other things so lovely, so beautiful, that my soul must have; I cannot leave them to go with You." He who died for you, He who left Heaven's glory in order to redeem your soul, calls to you and says, "Come with Me." Can you draw back and say, "No, it is too much to ask; I cannot leave these surroundings; I cannot leave these worldly follies; I cannot quit this place of danger for Your sake, Lord Jesus"? Surely there is not very much love there. You need to get down before Him and confess the sin of your cold-heartedness and indifference. You need to ask for a fresh vision of the love that He demonstrated in the cross that your heart may be weaned away from everything else. Dr. Watts has put it:

> He calls me from the lion's den,
>   From this wild world of beasts and men,
> To Zion where His glories are,
>   No Lebanon is half so fair.
> Nor dens of prey, nor flowery plains,
>   Nor earthly joys, nor earthly pains,
> Shall hold my feet or force my stay,
>   When Christ invites my soul away.

Does your heart respond to that? What He desires above everything else is to see His people finding satisfaction in His company.

You remember in the first chapter of this Song the bride said, looking up to the bridegroom, "We will remember thy love more than wine" (4). Now, in the closing verse of this section, he responds to her, saying, "How much better is thy love than wine! and the smell of thine ointments than all spices! Thy lips, O my spouse, drop as the honeycomb: honey and milk are under thy tongue; and the smell of thy garments is like the smell of Lebanon" (4:10-11). Christians should be fragrant with the sweetness of Christ. It is said of the disciples that the Jewish leaders "took knowledge...that they had been with Jesus." If we are in His company, there will be a rich fragrance of holiness, of heavenliness, about us wherever we are found.

A minister tells of riding with another preacher on the upper deck of a bus in London, England. As they came down a shabby street with a big factory on one side, they were halted, and they noticed the doors of the factory had opened and hundreds of girls were pouring out and making their way across the street to a lunch room. Suddenly the air was filled with a sweet delightful fragrance. The visitor said, "Isn't that remarkable in a factory district here in London? Such a wonderful fragrance! It seems like the odor of a great garden. You would not think of finding such fragrance in this district."

"Oh, you don't understand," said his friend; "this is one of the largest perfume factories in all the British Isles. These young people are working constantly among the perfumes, and everywhere they go the fragrance remains on their garments."

Beloved, if you and I are living in fellowship with Christ, if we keep in touch with Him, everywhere we go His fragrance will be exhibited in our lives.

In the final section of chapter 4 (verses 12-16) we have the individual believer, or Israel, or the church, whichever you will, pictured as a watered garden set apart for our Lord Himself to bring forth fruit that will be to His delight. Again we are shown the joyous privileges of those who are permitted to enter into communion with our blessed Lord.

This lovely figure is used on a number of other occasions in Scripture. In Isaiah 58:11, God pictured His people as such a garden: "The Lord shall guide thee continually, and satisfy thy soul in drought, and make fat thy bones: and thou shalt be like a watered garden, and like a spring of water, whose waters fail not." This beautiful picture refers primarily to Israel. Morally it speaks of any believer, and of that which God would see in all His saints as they walk with Him. In the book of the prophet Jeremiah we read,

> Therefore they shall come and sing in the height of Zion, and shall flow together to the goodness of the Lord, for wheat, and for wine, and for oil, and for the young of the flock and of the herd: and their soul shall be as a watered garden; and they shall not sorrow any more at all (Jeremiah 31:12).

It is the risen Christ Himself from whom we draw abundant supplies of mercy and grace, but did you ever think of your own heart as a garden in which He is to find His joy? Your very life is as a garden that exists for His pleasure. That is the figure given to us in this part of the Song. The bridegroom gazed upon his bride with his heart filled with delight as he said to her, "You are to be for me, you are like a lovely garden yielding its fruit and flowers for me, set apart for myself."

"A garden inclosed is my sister, my spouse; a spring shut up, a fountain sealed" (12). We in America like open gardens that anybody can enjoy, but in Syria and in other parts of the Middle East, many gardens are enclosed or walled in. This is necessary in some of those countries, as otherwise they would be destroyed by marauding creatures and robbers. It is as though the Lord says, "That is what I want My people to be, separated to Myself; I want them to have about them the wall of holiness, for I have marked them off as My own."

In Psalm 4:3 we read, "The Lord hath set apart him that is godly for himself." Some Christians shrink from the idea of separation. If it is only a legal thing, it may become mere Pharisaism with no heart to it. But if our separation is to Christ, if our soul is going out to Him and turning away from the world for love of Him, then separation is a very precious thing indeed. One does not need to think of it as legal bondage, for it is being set apart for God Himself. Could one think of a higher privilege on earth than that He might find His joy in us and we might find our joy in Him?

Satan likes to break down the wall, to destroy the principle of holy separation that would keep our hearts for the Lord alone. But what a loss it is to our own souls, and what a loss it means to Him, when His people become like a garden trodden under foot, as it were, by every wayfarer. That is what the Christian becomes who does not keep the path of separation.

Then notice the next figure, "A spring shut up, a fountain sealed." Pure water is a very precious thing in the East. Often, when a spring is discovered, it is walled about, covered, and locked. The owner of it keeps the key so that he can go and drink when he will, and the water is kept from pollution and waste. That is what our Lord would have in His people. He has given His Holy Spirit to dwell in us. The Holy Spirit is Himself the fountain of water within every believer's heart, that we might be to God's praise and glory. This living water within the garden will, of course, result in abundant fruit and flowers.

"Thy plants are an orchard of pomegranates, with pleasant fruits; camphire, with spikenard" (13). The orchard suggests more than a mere garden of beautiful flowers that are fair to look at, and fragrant to the senses. The orchard suggests fruitfulness as well. What precious fruit is borne by the believer; what precious fruit is found in the heart of the one who is sealed to God! In the letter to the Philippians, the apostle tells those dear saints that he is sure that God who has begun the good work in them will perform it until the day of Jesus Christ. He continues:

> And this I pray, that your love may abound yet more and more in knowledge and in all judgment; That ye may approve things that are excellent; that ye may be sincere and without offence till the day of Christ; Being filled with the fruits of righteousness, which are by Jesus Christ, unto the glory and praise of God (Philippians 1:9-11).

It seems to me that everyone ought to understand that a life lived for God produces the fruits of righteousness. Love, purity, goodness, sweetness, kindness, compassion, consideration for others, all of these things are the beautiful fruits that grow in this garden when the Living Water is properly fructifying the soil. In Galatians 5:22 we have a long list of the fruit of the Spirit. Challenge your own heart by asking, "Am I producing this kind of fruit for Him, 'Love, joy, peace, longsuffering'?" *Longsuffering* is that patience that makes you willing to endure. Then there is "gentleness, goodness, faith, meekness, and temperance." This is the delightful fruit that our Lord is looking for in the lives of His people. He would have every one of us as a garden that produces fruit like this.

The word translated "orchard" is really similar to the Persian word for *paradise*. It may suggest that just as God has a paradise above for His own people where they shall share His joy for all eternity, so a believer's heart in this world, when it is producing the fruit of the Spirit, is a paradise for God where He finds His joy and His delight. I wonder if we think enough of that side of our salvation. Are we not likely to become self-centered and merely consider God as serving us? We think of the blessed Lord Jesus giving Himself for us, dying for us, rising again for us, nurturing our souls, guiding us through the wilderness of this world and bringing us at last to glory. Some of the hymns we sing are almost entirely occupied with the blessings that come to us, but these do not rise to the height of the Christian's intimacy with God. It is when we are through thinking about what God is doing for us, and are seeking by grace to adore the One who does all this for us, and are letting our lives go out to Him as a thankoffering in praise and adoration, that we truly rise to the height of our Christian privileges. Then it is that He gathers these sweet and lovely fruits in His garden.

He gathers not only fruit on which He feeds, but also that which gives satisfaction in every sense: "Camphire, with spikenard, Spikenard and saffron; calamus and cinnamon, with all trees of frankincense; myrrh and aloes, with all the chief spices" (13-14). Some of these plants give forth their fragrance as the rain and dew fall on them; some of them emit a subtle aroma when the rays of the sun are warming them. Others never exude, never give out their fragrance until they are pierced and the sap flows from them. So it is with our lives. We need all kinds of varied experiences in order that we may exhibit the graces of Christ in our behavior. We are not only to be for His delight, but we are to be for His service too, in making known His grace to a lost world.

In the next verse we read, "A fountain of gardens, a well of living waters, and streams from Lebanon" (15). Let us see if we can correlate that. Lebanon is the backbone mountain range of Palestine, with mount Hermon to the north covered with snow. The streams coming down from Lebanon sink into the ground. As they do so, springs rise here and there in vales and dells to the surface of the earth; so the living water flows forth to refresh the thirsty soil. The living water represents, as we know from John's Gospel, the blessed Holy Spirit. Our Lord Jesus said,

> If any man thirst, let him come unto me, and drink. He that believeth on me, as the scripture hath said, out of his belly shall flow rivers of living water. (But this spake he of the Spirit, which they that believe on him should receive: for the Holy Ghost was not yet given; because that Jesus was not yet glorified) (John 7:37-39).

Now the Spirit of God descending from above enters into our inmost being and then we have the Living Water springing up to everlasting life. As our own hearts are refreshed and gladdened, the Living Water in abundance flows out from us for the blessing of a lost world around. Is this not a beautiful picture? My brother, my sister, what do you know of this life in the fullness of the Holy Spirit? Far too many of us seem to be content to know that our sins have been forgiven, and that we have a hope of Heaven based on some testimony that we have received from Holy Scripture. But it is more than this. We are not merely to have the assurance of our own salvation; every one of us should be as watered gardens for Him, with streams flowing out for the refreshment of dying men and women all about us.

In what measure is your life touching others? In what measure are you being used of God to win other souls for Christ? Many of us would have to confess that we have never had the privilege of winning one soul, that so far as we know we have never yet given a testimony to anyone that has really been blessed in his or her coming to Christ. Let me suggest that there must be something that is hindering the outflow of the Living Water. Can it be that great boulders of worldliness, selfishness, pride, carnality, sinful folly or covetousness are literally choking the fountain of Living Water, so that there is just a little trickling when there should be a wonderful outflowing? If this is the case, seek by grace to recognize these hindrances and deal with them one by one. Away with worldliness, away with pride. Who am I to be proud? What have I to be proud of? "What hast thou that thou didst not receive?" (1 Corinthians 4:7) Away with carnality, away with self-seeking, away with covetousness, away with living for my own interests; let me henceforth live for Him alone who shed His precious blood for me and redeemed me to Himself. As I thus deal with these things that hinder the outflow of the Living Water, I will myself enter into a new, living, blessed and wonderful experience. My testimony then will be a blessing to those around me, and my life will be at its best for Him.

As we move on to verse 16 of this chapter of the Song we note that there has been some question as to the identity of the first speaker in this verse. It is very evident that the one who speaks in the last sentence of this verse is the bride, but is it the bride or the bridegroom in the first part? "Awake, O north wind; and come, thou south; blow upon my garden, that the spices thereof may flow out." If it is the bridegroom who is speaking, then he is calling on the winds to blow on what he calls, "my garden"—the heart of his bride—in order that she may be at her best for him. If, on the other hand, as I am personally inclined to believe, it is the bride who is speaking, then it indicates her yearning desire to be all that he would have her to be. Dear child of God, is that your desire? Do you yearn to be all that Christ would have you to be? Or are you still actuated by worldly and selfish motives that hinder communion with Him?

Listen to these words again, as we think of them as coming from the lips of the bride, "Awake, O north wind." That is the cold, bitter, biting, wintry blast. Naturally she would shrink from that as we all would; yet the cold of winter is as necessary as the warmth of summer if there is going to be perfection in fruit-bearing. It is as though she says, "Blessed God, if need be, let Your Spirit breathe on me through trial and sorrow, difficulty and perplexity; take from me all in which I have trusted from the human standpoint; bereave me of everything if You so will; leave me cold, naked, and alone except for Your love, but work out Your will in me."

The best apples are grown in northern climates where frost and cold have to be faced. Those grown in semi-tropical countries are apt to be tasteless and insipid. It takes the cold to bring out the flavor. And it is so with our lives. We need the north winds of adversity and trial as well as the zephyrs of the south that are so agreeable to our natures. The very things we shrink from are the experiences that will work in us to produce the peaceable fruits of righteousness. If everything were easy and soft and beautiful in our lives, they would be empty. There would be so little in them that could delight God's heart, and so there must be the north wind as well as the south. But on the other hand, we need the south wind also, and our precious Lord tempers the winds to every one of us. It is a blessed thing to be in that state of soul where we can just trust ourselves to Him.

Charles Spurgeon tells of a man who had the words, "God is love," painted on his weathervane. Someone said, "That is a strange text to put there. Do you mean to say that God's love is as changeable as the wind?" "Oh no," said the other; "I mean that whichever way the wind blows, God is love." Do not forget that. It may be the north wind of bereavement when your dearest and best are snatched from you, but "God is love." It may be that the cold wind of what the world calls ill-fortune will sweep away like a fearful cyclone all that you have accumulated for years, but "God is love." It is written, "The Lord hath his way in the whirlwind and in the storm, and the clouds are the dust of his feet" (Nahum 1:3).

Perhaps you have been asking questions like this, "Why has God allowed the sufferings we have had to undergo? Why has He allowed these weeks and months with no employment and everything slipping away, the savings of years gone?" Dear child of God, He does not give account of any of His matters now. But, "When you stand with Christ in glory, / Looking o'er life's finished story," then He will make it clear to you, and you will know why He allowed the cold wind to blow over His garden as well as the south wind. If you would bow to Him now and recognize His unchanging love, perhaps He would be able to trust you with more zephyrs from the south than you ordinarily experience. We are not subject enough to the will of God. We need to learn the lesson that, "All things work together for good to them that love God, to them who are the called according to his purpose" (Romans 8:28).

"Awake, O north wind; and come, thou south; blow upon my garden, that the spices thereof may flow out." In other words, "Anything, Lord, that will make me a better Christian, a more devoted saint; anything that will make me a more faithful child of Yours, so that You can find Your delight in me." Is that your thought? And then the bride looked up into the face of her bridegroom and said, "Let my beloved come into his garden, and eat his pleasant fruits" (16). How He delights to get such an invitation as that from His people.

SONG OF SOLOMON

CHAPTER 5

I opened to my beloved;
but my beloved had withdrawn himself, and was gone (6).

In the first verse of chaper 5 we read the bridegroom's immediate response to the bride's invitation to enter his garden. This verse really belongs to the previous chapter. She no sooner says, "Come," than he replies, "I am come into my garden, my sister, my spouse: I have gathered my myrrh with my spice; I have eaten my honeycomb with my honey; I have drunk my wine with my milk: eat, O friends; drink, yea, drink abundantly, O beloved" (1).

The scene closes with rapturous communion. And when you look up to the Beloved of your heart and say, "Come into Thy garden and eat Thy pleasant fruits," He will immediately respond, "I am come." You will never have to wait; you will never have to give Him a second invitation. If you have any time for Him, He always has time for you.

The rest of Song of Solomon 5 is a part of a longer section that concludes with the fifth verse of chapter 8. In that entire portion we have traced out for us in a very wonderful way the interruption of communion and its final restoration. We have already had one similar picture in this book where the bridegroom's absence produced a temporary sense of estrangement (chapter 3). We have that dealt with more fully in this section, where the bridegroom's advances are coldly spurned. Remember that the bride represents any regenerated soul and that the bridegroom is our blessed Lord Jesus Christ.

If we keep this in mind we should have no difficulty in getting the spiritual lesson of these chapters.

We have all known such periods of glad joy in the Lord as those described in Song of Solomon 4. But how often have we found that, following almost immediately on a period of great blessing and delightful fellowship with the Lord, there may come a time of spiritual dearth and broken fellowship? We have all experienced interrupted communion. You recall that in Israel's history they were scarcely through rejoicing over the wonderful victory at Jericho before they were wringing their hands in despair because of the defeat at Ai. Often in our Christian lives we have similar experiences. Perhaps you go to an edifying meeting where your whole soul is stirred by the singing, by the prayers, and by the ministry of the Word; you feel as though you would never again lose sight of your blessed Redeemer's face. Yet the spirit is willing but the flesh is weak, and within a very short time you find yourself inquiring, "Where is the blessedness I knew / When first I saw the Lord?" Everything seems dark and cloudy and you no longer discern your Savior's presence. Is there any one who has had uninterrupted communion with the Lord throughout all the years? I am sure there is not. Even if we imagined so, it would simply be because we lacked the sensitivity to recognize that our behavior has grieved Him.

As we continue our narrative we see that the bride has retired and she is just about asleep, yet a bit restless, when there comes a knock at the door. It is the knock of the beloved one who has returned from a distant journey. He cries, "Open to me, my sister, my love, my dove, my undefiled: for my head is filled with dew, and my locks with the drops of the night" (2). This is a wonderfully beautiful picture. We have the same picture in the New Testament in the third chapter of the book of Revelation. We see the Lord Jesus waiting outside the door of the Laodicean church. He says, "Behold, I stand at the door, and knock: if any man hear my voice, and open the door, I will come in to him, and will sup with him, and he with me" (20). But what lethargy there is! How few respond to His gracious request! And so here the bride exclaims, "I have put off my coat; how shall I put it on? I have washed my feet; how shall

I defile them?" (3) There is a fretfulness in her response: *Why am I disturbed at this hour? Why did you not come at some other time? I have taken off my coat; why should I put it on now? I have washed my feet; why should I dirty them?* This refers to the eastern custom of washing the feet before seeking repose, for in that land they wore sandals and the upper part of the foot had no covering. In other words, she did not want to bestir herself even so much as to open the door to him.

Have you ever known similar experiences? Have you ever been so much concerned with your own affairs, with seeking your own self-pleasing ease, that when His voice called you for an hour of communion and fellowship with Him, you really repelled His advances? Instead, you should have gladly thrown open the door and said, "Blessed Lord, nothing else is worthwhile but to enjoy the sunshine of Your smile, to enjoy fellowship with You."

In this instance, we see in the bride's behavior evidence of this lackadaisical attitude. But then, as she lies there dozing, neither actually asleep nor awake, she discerns something that moves her heart. She says, "My beloved put in his hand by the hole of the door" (4). We will not understand the simile unless we are familiar with those eastern doors and locks. The lock was on the inside of the door. There was an opening where the owner, if he had the key, could reach in and use the key from the inside to open the door. The bridegroom comes, but he does not open the door in that way. He has asked admission and wants her to rise and open for him. She sees that hand come through the opening. The moment she does so, her heart is stirred and she cries, "Oh, I must let him in." Then she rises and hurries to the door.

As she lays hold of the lock, she exclaims, "My hands dropped with myrrh, and my fingers with sweet smelling myrrh, upon the handles of the lock" (5). That refers to another eastern custom. When a lover came to visit the one who had won his heart and found she was not at home, or though at home she refused his advances, he covered the lock of the door with sweet-smelling ointments and left flowers as a token of his affection. And so the bride says, "My hands dropped with myrrh, and my fingers with sweet smelling myrrh." It was not a dream then; he had really been there and had gone. She threw the door open to enable him to hear her cry, "Come, come in!" but there was no answering response. "My beloved," she said, "had withdrawn himself and was gone" (6).

Love is very sensitive. The trouble with many of us is that we fail to recognize this. We have an idea that the beloved one should be ready whenever we are for a time of gladness together, but that is not always so. Sometimes when He comes to the heart's door we practically say, "No; it is inconvenient. I do not want to drop things right now." But later when we would enjoy His presence we find He has gone. Have you ever had such experiences? Has He come to you and said, "I want you to sit down with Me over My Word; I want you to spend a little time in prayer, to dismiss other things from your mind and commune with Me." Have you said, "Oh, but I have so much to occupy me; I cannot do it now"? Plenty of time for self but very little for Him. And then some wonderful token of His lovingkindness came to you, and you said, "Oh, I must respond to His heart." You threw open the door as it were and called, but He was not there. And did you ever know what it was to go on for days and weeks without any real sense of His presence? "My beloved had withdrawn himself." If you do not respond to His voice when He comes to you in tender grace, you may seek Him for a long time before you will enjoy fellowship with Him again. Such is the sensitiveness of love. He wants to make you feel that His love is worthwhile. He wants to test you as to whether you are really in earnest when you profess to desire fellowship with Him.

As the story goes on, the bride leaves the house and goes out into the city seeking after her beloved. She makes her way from street to street, calling his name, looking here and there and wondering where he has hidden himself. She says, "The watchmen that went about the city found me, they smote me, they wounded me; the keepers of the walls took away my veil from me" (7). You will always have to suffer if you refuse obedience to the voice of Christ when He calls you. You will always have to be tested before communion is restored.

There is a word in the New Testament that has troubled some

believers. In 1 Corinthians 11 we are told that a Christian woman, when she is engaged in worship with the people of God or in public prayer or testimony, is to cover her head. People ask, "Why the covering?" The Bible says that the covering is her "power" (10, KJV). Does that seem like a strange word to use? I believe Song of Solomon 5:7 sheds some light on this. The covering on the head of the bride was her power. In what sense? Look at it this way. As long as her head was veiled she was considered a chaste and modest wife or maiden and that was her power. But when the keepers saw her going about the streets at night, they misunderstood her motive and character, and they took away her veil. The unveiled woman was marked out as one who was unclean and unchaste.

Years ago I was a Salvation Army officer. I remember that our Army girls could go anywhere with those little blue bonnets. I never knew but one in all the years I was connected with them, who was insulted by any one in any place as long as she wore that little bonnet. I have been seeking the lost in the lowest kind of dives on the Barbary Coast of San Francisco and have seen the Army girls come in with their literature and go from one rough ungodly man to another. Ordinarily no one ever said an unkind or a wicked word to them. But once a drunken sailor dared to say something insulting to one of them, immediately practically the entire crowd jumped on him. They knocked him down and gave him such a trouncing as he had never had before. Then they threw him into the street for the police to pick up. The little blue bonnet was the power of the Salvation Army woman, as was the veil that covered the head of the woman in that oriental land.

The uncovered head indicated an immoral woman, while the covered head was the power of the moral woman. The covering marked her as one seeking to live a life of goodness and purity. So here, in the Song, because the bride has lost the sense of her bridegroom's presence, she is branded as though she were impure and unholy. This shame has come on her because she did not immediately respond to her bridegroom's call.

She turns for help to the daughters of Jerusalem as the morning dawns and she sees them coming down the street. "I charge you, O daughters of Jerusalem, if ye find my beloved, that ye tell him, that I am sick of love" (8). In other words, "Tell him my heart is yearning for him; tell him I repent of my indifference, of my cold-heartedness and my unconcern, and want him above everything else." Christian, is that what your heart says? Are you a backslidden believer? Do you remember times when you enjoyed communion with your Lord, when life with Him was sweet and precious, but that fellowship was broken, and you are saying with Job, "Oh that I knew where I might find him"? (Job 23:3) Does your heart say today, "Tell Him that I am sick with love, that my whole being is yearning after Him; I want to be restored to Him, to the sweetness of communion"?

The daughters of Jerusalem say, "What is thy beloved more than another beloved, O thou fairest among women? what is thy beloved more than another beloved, that thou dost so charge us?" (5:9) In other words, "This one that you say means so much to you, why is he more to you than you might expect another to be to us?" The world says, "Why is Christ more to you than any other? Why does Jesus mean so much more to you than the things of the world? Tell us that we may seek Him with you."

Then at once the bride begins to praise her bridegroom. From verse ten to the end of the chapter in wonderful oriental imagery she extols his kindness, his graciousness, his aptness to help, his strength, and his tenderness. She cries, "My beloved is...the chiefest among ten thousand" (10).

SONG OF SOLOMON

CHAPTERS 6–7

I am my beloved's,
and my beloved is mine (6:3).

As we look at these two chapters we are reminded that they are part of a larger section describing the interruption in the relationship between the bride and bridegroom, followed by the exultant reuniting of chapter 8.

As chapter 5 closes, the bride, in search of her lover, is describing him in glorious terms. And when she thus praises him her friends turn again and say, "Whither is thy beloved gone, O thou fairest among women? whither is thy beloved turned aside? that we may seek him with thee" (6:1). In other words, "Where has he gone? How is it that you have let him slip out of your sight if he is so much to you?" Is that not a proper question? If Christ is so precious to you, if He means so much to you, why is it that you so easily allow fellowship to be broken? Why do you so readily permit other things to come in and hinder communion?

And then instantly as she bears testimony to him, she recalls the last words he said to her before that eventful night, "I am come into my garden" (5:1). Her own heart was the garden—she knows where he is. She says, "My beloved is gone down into his garden, to the beds of spices, to feed in the gardens, and to gather lilies" (6:2). And instantly he speaks; he is right there. He had been waiting and watching for her to come to the place where he was everything to her soul. At once he exclaims, "Thou art beautiful, O my love, as

Tirzah, comely as Jerusalem, terrible as an army with banners" (4). And then through all the rest of the chapter he praises her. He expresses his appreciation of her as she had expressed hers of him.

In chapter seven, verses 1-9, the bridegroom uses one beautiful figure after another to tell all his delight in her. It is a wonderful thing to know that the Lord has far more delight in His people than we ourselves have ever had in Him. Some day we will enjoy Him to the fullest. Some day He will be everything to us. But as long as we are here, we never appreciate Him as much as He appreciates us. As she listens to his expression of love, her heart is assured; she has the sense of restoration and fellowship. In verse ten she says, "I am my beloved's, and his desire is toward me." In other words, he has not turned against her. When we turn from Him, the natural thought of our hearts is that He has turned against us, but He has not. If He allows us to go through trial, it is like Joseph testing his brethren in order to see if there was genuine repentance of sin.

Three times in this little book we have similar expressions to this, "I am my beloved's, and his desire is toward me." In 2:16 we read, "My beloved is mine, and I am his." That is very precious. Are you able to say, "My beloved is mine, and I am His?" In other words, Have you given yourself to Him? Have you trusted Him as your Savior? If you have, He has given Himself to you. Just the very moment you give yourself to Him in faith, that moment He gives Himself to you and comes to dwell in your heart. This is the assurance of salvation: Christ is mine, and I am His. And then in 6:3, she says, "I am my beloved's, and my beloved is mine." That is communion. I belong to him and he belongs to me, that we may enjoy one another together. And then in 7:10 we read, "I am my beloved's, and his desire is toward me." Every doubt and every fear is gone. She has found her satisfaction in him and he finds his in her. What a wonderful picture of the communion between the Christian and his Savior.

Is this only a picture, or is it a reality in our lives? Is it not a fact that so often we do the very things the Shulamite did? So often we turn a deaf ear to the Bridegroom's voice. We can be so busy even with Christian work that we do not take time for Him. I can be so occupied with preaching that I do not have time for prayer. I can be so taken up with preparing sermons that I do not have time to feed on the Word. You may ask, "Why, how can you prepare sermons without feeding on the Word?" It is one thing to study the Bible in order to prepare an address that I am to give to other people. It is another thing to sit down quietly in the presence of the Lord and say, "Blessed Savior, as I open Your Book I want to hear Your voice speaking to my heart. I want You to talk to me, to express Yourself to me in tones of tender love." As I read His Word in that attitude, He speaks to my soul; as I lift my heart to Him in prayer, I talk with Him. That is communion.

Do not be content with the knowledge of salvation; do not be content to know that your soul is eternally secure; do not be content to know that you are serving Him in some little measure. Remember, there is something that means more to Him than all your service, and that is to sit at His feet and delight your soul in His love. As you read again the bride's description of her bridegroom in the fifth chapter it will remind you of the fullness there is in Christ. It seems as though every figure is exhausted to show His wonder.

> Join all the glorious names
>   Of wisdom, love, and power,
> That ever mortals knew,
>   That angels ever bore;
> All are too poor to speak His worth,
> Too poor to set my Saviour forth.
>   Isaac Watts

Oh, to have the heart so occupied with Him that we lose sight of everything else, and Christ alone will satisfy every longing of our souls!

SONG OF SOLOMON

CHAPTER 8

Many waters cannot quench love,
neither can the floods drown it (7).

Throughout this little book we have been tracing the evidence of the love of the bridegroom for his bride, from the time when the shepherd first looked on the shepherdess and his heart went out to her until the time when they were united in marriage. It is a beautiful picture, first of the love of Christ reaching us in our deep, deep need, and then the glorious union with Him, which will be consummated at the marriage supper of the Lamb.

In verse 6 of this chapter you hear the bride exclaiming, "Set me as a seal upon thine heart, as a seal upon thine arm." The seal represents something that is final and settled. One draws up a legal document and seals it and that settles it. And so Christ and His loved ones have entered into an eternal relationship, and He has given us the seal, the Holy Spirit. "In whom also after that ye believed, ye were sealed with that holy Spirit of promise, Which is the earnest of our inheritance until the redemption of the purchased possession" (Ephesians 1:13-14). That seal is the pledge of His love. You will notice that in the words that follow verse 6 we have love spoken of in four ways, at least we have four characteristics of love.

First, there is the *strength* of love. "Love is strong as death." Second, the *jealousy* of love. In the King James version we read, "Jealousy is cruel as the grave." Human love may be a very cruel thing indeed. But actually the word translated "cruel" is the ordinary Hebrew word for *firm* or *unyielding*. It may be translated, "Jealousy is unyielding as the grave." "The coals thereof are coals of fire, which hath a most vehement flame." This expression, "a vehement flame," in the Hebrew text is "a flame of Jah." That is the first part of the name of Jehovah and it is one of the titles of God. In the third place we have the *endurance* of love: "Many waters cannot quench love, neither can the floods drown it" (7). And then lastly, there is the *value* of love: "If a man would give all the substance of his house for love, it would utterly be contemned" (7).

First let us meditate on the strength of love. We are thinking, of course, of the love of our God as revealed in the Lord Jesus Christ, for Christ is the Bridegroom of our souls. "Love is strong as death." This He has already demonstrated: "Christ also loved the church, and gave himself for it" (Ephesians 5:25). Giving Himself meant going into death to redeem His own. "Love is strong as death." We might even say in His case, "It is stronger than death," for death could not quench His love. He went down into death and came up in triumph that He might make us His own.

We are reminded of the strength of His love as we gather at the Lord's table. He wishes us to cherish His death and resurrection in a special way when we come together to remember Him. He knows how apt we are to forget. He knows how easy it is to be occupied with the ordinary things of life, and even with the work of the Lord, and forget for the moment the price He paid for our redemption. He would call us back from time to time to sit together in sweetest and most solemn fellowship and meditate on that mighty love of His which is "strong as death." Nothing could turn Him aside.

> Love that no thought can reach,
> Love that no tongue can teach,
> Matchless it is!

Because there was no other way to redeem our souls, "And...the time was come that he should be received up, he stedfastly set his face to go to Jerusalem" (Luke 9:51). When He went through that Samaritan village, they did not receive Him because they realized that there was no desire on His part to remain among them at that time. They saw "his face...as though he would go to Jerusalem," (53) and they said as it were, "Well, if He prefers to go to Jerusalem rather than remain here with us, we are not going to pay attention to His message. We are not interested in the proclamation that He brings." How little they understood that it was for them, as truly as for the Jews in Judea, that He "stedfastly set his face to go to Jerusalem." If He had not gone to Jerusalem and given Himself up to the death of the cross, there could be no salvation for Samaritan, Jew, or Gentile. But oh, the strength of His love! He allowed nothing to divert Him from that purpose for which He had come from Heaven. Before He left the glory, He said, "Lo, I come (in the volume of the book it is written of me,) to do thy will, O God" (Hebrews 10:7). For Him to do the will of God meant laying down His life on the cross for our redemption. Do we think of it as much as we should? Do we give ourselves to meditation, to dwelling on the love of Christ, a love that passeth knowledge? Do we often say to ourselves, "The Son of God...loved me, and gave himself for me" (Galatians 2:20)? Oh, the strength of His love!

Then we think of the jealousy of love. I know that jealousy in these sinful hearts of ours is often a most contemptible and despicable thing. Jealousy on our part generally means utter selfishness. We are so completely selfish, we do not like to share anything we consider valuable with anyone else. What untold sorrow has come into many a home because of the unreasonable jealousy of a husband, of a wife, of parents, or of children. But while we deprecate a jealousy that has selfishness and sin at the root of it, there is another jealousy that is absolutely pure and holy. Even on our lower plane someone has well said that, "Love is only genuine as long as it is jealous." When the husband reaches the place where he says, "I do not care how my wife bestows her favors on others; I do not care how much she runs around with other men; I am so large-hearted I can share her with everybody," that husband does not love his wife. If you could imagine a wife talking like that about her husband, you would know that love was gone, that it was dead.

Love cannot but be jealous, but let us see that it is a jealousy that is free from mere selfishness and unwarranted suspicion. When we think of it in connection with God we remember that one of the first things we learned to recite was the Ten Commandments, and some of us were perplexed when we read, "I the Lord thy God am a jealous God, visiting the iniquity of the fathers upon the children unto the third and fourth generation of them that hate me" (Exodus 20:5). We shrank back from that because we were so used to thinking of jealousy as a despicable human passion, that we could not think of God having it in His character. But it is He who has a right to be jealous. God's jealousy is as pure as is His love, and it is because He loves us so tenderly that He is jealous. In what sense is He jealous? God knows that our souls' happiness and blessing can only be found in walking in fellowship with Himself. He loves us so much He does not want to see us turning away from the enjoyment of His love and trying to find satisfaction in any lesser affection, which can only be for harm and eventual ruin. "The end of those things is death" (Romans 6:21).

Paul writing to the Corinthian church said, "I am jealous over you with a godly jealousy; for I have espoused you to one husband, that I may present you as a chaste virgin to Christ" (2 Corinthians 11:2). Then he gave the ground of his jealousy: "But I fear, lest by any means, as the serpent beguiled Eve through his subtilty, so your minds should be corrupted from the simplicity that is in Christ" (3). You see Paul was a true pastor. He loved the people of Christ's flock and knew that their only lasting joy was to be found in living in communion with their Savior. His heart was torn with a holy jealousy if he saw them turning aside to the things of the world, following after the things of the flesh, or being ensnared by the devil. Every God-anointed pastor will feel that way.

Young believers sometimes imagine that some of us who try to lead the flock of God are often needlessly hard and severe. They think we are unsympathetic and lacking in compassion and tenderness when we earnestly warn them of the folly of worldliness and carnality. They say, "Oh, they don't understand. That old fogy preacher, I have no doubt, had his fling when he was young. Now he is old and these things no longer interest him, and so he wants to keep us from having a good time!"

Let me "speak as a fool," and yet I trust to the glory of God. As a young believer coming to Christ when I was fourteen years old, the first lesson I had to learn was that there is nothing in this poor world that could satisfy my heart. By the grace of God I sought to give it all up for Jesus' sake. The only regret I have today is that there have ever been times in my life when I have drifted into carnality and fallen into a low backslidden state. I regret that I allowed myself something that afterward left a bad conscience and a sense of broken fellowship. I never was happy until it was judged, and I was once more in communion with the Lord. If sometimes we speak strongly to you, young believer, about following the ways of the world, reminding you that God has said, "Come out from among them, and be ye separate,...and touch not the unclean thing" (2 Corinthians 6:17), it is because we have learned by years of experience that there is no peace, there is no lasting joy, there is no true unspoiled happiness for those who walk in the ways of the world. If you want a life of gladness, a life of enduring bliss; if you want to be able to lie down at last and face death with a glad, free spirit, then we beg of you, follow the path that your blessed Lord Jesus took. Oh, that we might not be turned aside but that we might rouse our souls to a godly jealousy.

I wonder if you have ever noticed that the blessed Holy Spirit who dwells in every believer is Himself spoken of as jealous. There is a passage found in James 4:4-5, that I am afraid is not often really understood, because of the way it is translated in the King James version. Yet it is a very striking passage:

> Ye adulterers and adulteresses, know ye not that the friendship of the world is enmity with God? whosoever therefore will be a friend of the world is the enemy of God. Do ye think that the scripture saith in vain, The spirit that dwelleth in us lusteth to envy?

Take that to your heart, dear young Christian. Do not be seduced by the world and its folly; do not be turned aside from the path of faithfulness to Christ by the mad rush for worldly pleasure and amusement; do not allow the flesh to turn you away and rob you of

what should be your chief joy. "The friendship of the world is en-
mity with God. whosoever therefore will be a friend of the world is
the enemy of God." It is the next verse that perhaps we might not
understand. "Do ye think that the scripture saith in vain, The spirit
that dwelleth in us lusteth to envy?" One might gather that this expression, "The spirit that dwelleth in us lusteth to envy," was a quo-
tation from Scripture, as though He were asking, "Do you think the
Scripture, that is, the Old Testament, saith in vain, 'The spirit that
dwelleth in us lusteth to envy?' " But you can search the Old Testament from the beginning of Genesis to the end of Malachi, and you
will not find those words or anything that sounds like them. So it is
clear that that is not what is meant. In fact, there are really two
distinct questions in the Greek. First there is the question, "Do ye
think that the scripture speaketh in vain?" Do you? Having read its
warnings and its admonitions against worldliness, against being
unequally yoked, against pursuing the pleasures of sin, against following the path of the flesh, do you sometimes say in your heart, "I
know it is all in the Bible, but after all, I am not going to take it too
seriously?" Do you think that the Scripture speaks this warning in
vain?

Why has God put these things in His Word? Is it because He
does not love you and desires to keep you from things that would
do you good? That is what the devil told Eve in the beginning. He
insinuated that God did not love her. He said, "God doth know that
in the day ye eat thereof, then your eyes shall be opened, and ye
shall be as gods, knowing good and evil" (Genesis 3:5). And Eve
said in effect, "I am going to eat of it; I will try anything once." Is
that what you have been saying too? If you can only do this or do
that, you think you will have an experience you have never had
before. The whole world is looking for new thrills today. Before
you act, put the question to yourself, "Does the Scripture speak in
vain?" It tells you that the end of all these things is death and you
may be assured the Scripture does not speak in vain.

Then there is a second question in that passage in James 4, "[Doth]
The Spirit that dwelleth in us [jealously desire]?" And the answer
is, "Yes." The Holy Ghost dwelling in the believer jealously de-

sires to keep us away from the world and to keep our hearts true to Christ. Do you realize that you never tried to go into anything that dishonored the Lord, you never took a step to go into the world, but the Spirit of God within you was grieved? He sought to exercise you because He jealously desired to keep you faithful to Christ. I am talking to Christians. If you are not a Christian, the Spirit does not dwell in you.

Our blessed Lord wants you all for Himself. People say sometimes, "Well, I want to give the Lord the first place in my heart," and they mean that there will be a lot of places for other things. The Lord does not merely want the first place. He wants the whole place; He wants to control your whole heart, and when He has the entire control, everything you do will be done for His glory.

A striking little incident is told by Pastor Dolman. Before World War I he was in Russia holding some meetings in the palace of one of the Russian nobility. Among those who attended the meetings was a grand duchess. She was a sincere evangelical Christian. Dr. Dolman was talking one day about a life devoted to Christ, about separation and unworldliness. When he finished, the grand duchess stepped forward and said, "I do not agree with everything Pastor Dolman said."

"What did I say with which you do not agree, Your Imperial Highness?" asked Dr. Dolman.

"You said it is wrong to go to the theater. I go to the theater; but I never go without first getting down on my knees and asking Him to go with me, and He does."

Pastor Dolman said, "But, Your Imperial Highness, I did not say a word about the theater."

"I know; but you meant that."

"Your Imperial Highness," said Dr. Dolman, "are you not turning things around? Who gave you or me authority to decide where we will go or what we will do, and then to ask the Lord to be with us in it? Instead of getting down on your knees and saying, 'Lord, I am going to the theater, come with me,' why don't you wait until He comes to you and says, 'Grand Duchess, I am going to the theater, and I want you to go with Me?'"

She threw up her hands and was honest enough to say, "Pastor Dolman, you have spoiled the theater for me. I cannot go again."

"Where He leads me, I will follow," but don't you start and ask Him to tag along. Let Him lead. Because He knows that your real, lasting happiness and joy are bound up in devotion to Him, He is jealous lest you should be turned aside.

Next we notice the endurance of love. "Many waters cannot quench love, neither can the floods drown it" (Song of Solomon 8:7). How precious that is! How blessedly this was proven by Christ. He went down beneath the floods of divine judgment. He could say, "Deep calleth unto deep at the noise of thy waterspouts: all thy waves and thy billows are gone over me" (Psalm 42:7). But it did not quench His love. Through all the years since His people have had to endure many things—they have had to pass through deep waters, to go through great trials—but He has been with them through it all. "In all their affliction he was afflicted, and the angel of his presence saved them" (Isaiah 63:9). In Isaiah 43:2 we read, "When thou passest through the waters, I will be with thee; and through the rivers, they shall not overflow thee: when thou walkest through the fire, thou shalt not be burned; neither shall the flame kindle upon thee." Don't you love to have somebody to whom you can go with all your troubles and know He will never get tired of you?

Some years ago I became acquainted with a poor little old lady in a place where I was ministering the Word. She was going through all kinds of sorrow, and she came to me and said, "I would just like to tell you about my troubles." I felt like saying, "Dear sister, I wish you would tell them to the Lord." But I sat down and listened. Now for over ten years I have been getting her troubles by mail, and I try to send her a little encouraging and sympathetic word in reply. Recently I met her again and she said, "You must be getting awfully tired of my troubles." If I had told the truth, I would have had to say, "Yes, I am;" but I said, "What is troubling you now?" "Oh," she said, "it is not anything new, but it is such a comfort to find somebody who will listen to my trials and understand!" And she was so effusive in her gratitude I was ashamed that I had not entered into things more deeply.

We have a great High Priest who never wearies of our trials. We weary of hearing of them sometimes because they stir our hearts and we would like to do that which we cannot do; but He has power to see us through. No trial, no distress, can quench His love. "Having loved his own which were in the world, he loved them unto the end" (John 13:1). Somebody translated this verse this way, "Having loved His own which were in the world, He loved them all the way through." Through what? Through everything. He even loved Peter through his denial, through his cursing and swearing, and loved him back into fellowship with Himself. His love is unfailing. Having taken us up in grace, He loves to the end.

Let us look now at the value of love. Can you purchase love? Can you pay for it? I was in a home at one time where a very rich man of seventy years of age, worth millions, had married a girl of eighteen. Her ambitious, worldly-minded mother had engineered the marriage. I could not help noticing that young wife off in a corner sobbing to herself and crying bitterly. I tried never to interfere, for I did not want her to tell me what was in her heart.

One day the husband said, "Do you notice how downhearted my wife is?" I said, "She must have had some great sorrow." "I am her sorrow," he said. "She was a poor girl, very beautiful and talented, and as you know I have been very successful. I just thought that I could give her every comfort and could surely make her love me. I know that we do not seem to be suited; she is so much younger than I. But she can have everything, all the beautiful clothes and jewels she wants; surely any girl ought to be happy in a home like this. But, you know, it is all in vain; I cannot seem to buy her love."

Of course not. He ought to have known that he did not have in his heart that to which she could respond. They belonged to two different ages, as it were. "Many waters cannot quench love, neither can the floods drown it: if a man would give all the substance of his house for love, it would utterly be contemned." You cannot buy love, but oh, His love to us creates love in us. It is not the wonderful things that He has done for us, it is not the fact that He has enriched us for eternity, but it is because of what He is. "We love him, because he first loved us" (1 John 4:19).

His is an unchanging love,
Higher than the heights above;
Deeper than the depths beneath,
Free and faithful, strong as death.

What a blessed thing to know Him and love Him and be loved by Him! Oh, to be kept from wounding such a Lover, from grieving His Holy Spirit! For we read, "The love of God is shed abroad in our hearts by the Holy Ghost which is given unto us" (Romans 5:5).

After the bride in the Song of Solomon had been brought into the full enjoyment of the privileges that the bridegroom delighted to lavish on her, she remembered with concern her sister back home: "What shall we do for our sister?" (8:8) The bridegroom had first encountered his bride as a shepherdess there in the hill country. He loved her and won her heart in those trying days when she felt herself so despised and neglected. She was brought to the palace and united in marriage to the king. Enjoying to the full his tender consideration and surrounded by the evidences of his affection, she could not keep from thinking of the little mountain home from which she had come.

She thought of the dear old mother who had raised her and cared for her after the father's death, for it is evident that the mother was a widow. The family earned a precarious living by overseeing the king's vineyard. Then she thought of the little sister, much younger than she, who had none of the privileges that she was enjoying. And as she thought of her, she seemed to say, "This bridegroom of mine, my king, the one who has loved me and brought me into these privileges, cannot but take an interest in my family, in my household, and I am going to speak to him about that sister of mine." And so she turned to him in the most tender and confiding way, and said, "I have a little sister, a little undeveloped sister, up there in the vineyard. I am concerned about her. Is there not something we could do for her? What shall we do for our sister?"

He responded at once, "If she be a wall, we will build upon her a palace of silver: and if she be a door, we will inclose her with boards of cedar" (9). You see, this is just the oriental way of saying, "I am so glad you spoke to me about that little sister of yours; I am so glad that you have not forgotten her and her needs. It will be a real privilege for me to show my love for you by what I do for her." And so he used the striking figures of the wall and the door as he asserted his willingness to help. It was as though he said, "Whatever her circumstances are, and whatever her needs are, I will be delighted to minister to them and I will make you my agent in doing it."

It seems to me this expresses one of the very first evidences of union with Christ. We are no sooner saved ourselves, no sooner rejoicing in the knowledge of Christ as our Redeemer, as the Lover of our souls, as our heavenly Bridegroom, than we begin to think of others less privileged. Our hearts cry out with longing, "What about my little sister? What about my brother? What about those who are still in their sins and still in their deep, deep need, who do not know or understand Your incomprehensible love that means so much to me?" It is the Holy Spirit Himself who puts that yearning into our hearts that leads us to show an interest in the souls of others. In other words, every real Christian feels within him something that impels him to missionary service.

Are you saved? Then have you been to the Lord about that little sister, or about that neglected brother? Perhaps it is a little sister or a brother you have never seen, and maybe from an altogether different nation. Perhaps that little sister of yours is far away—a child-widow in India, a down-trodden native woman in central Africa, or a degraded Indian in the wilds of South America—yet they are your sisters, for we read, God "hath made of one blood all nations of men for to dwell on all the face of the earth" (Acts 17:26). You may say, "But she is so sinful, so undeserving." Have you forgotten that you too were sinful and undeserving and the grace that is lavished on you came from His heart of love? He delights to give to the undeserving. The very need of that little sister of yours is the reason why you should be going to the Lord about her.

The bride here is really praying for her sister. Do you often go to the blessed Lord in prayer for that sister of yours? Perhaps it is a brother. You who rejoice in Christ Jesus, do you think very often of that poor, ignorant, under-privileged, degraded, sinful brother of yours? Perhaps he is living in pagan darkness today, or dwelling in the slums of one of our great cities, or he may be enjoying all that this life has to offer and yet not knowing Christ? Have you spoken to God in behalf of that degraded one? Somebody has said, "A selfish Christian is a contradiction in terms;" yet we do hear people talking about selfish Christians. Christianity is the demonstration of the love of Christ in one's life. The same love that was lavished on you He would now have you lavish on others in their need. We are given wonderful illustrations of this principle throughout Scripture.

In John 1 we read how the Lord revealed Himself to one and another, and every one who got that divine revelation went after someone else. Each said in effect, "I have a brother, a friend, a dear one in need, and I must go to that one and tell the story of Jesus; tell him that we have found Him." The privileges and blessings that God has given to us in Christ are not given to us for ourselves alone. We may say in connection with them all: You must either use them or lose them. "What," you say, "are you telling us that we may lose our souls after having been truly converted?" Your soul is not a blessing; it is you. Of course you cannot lose that if it is saved. I recognize the fact that having life eternal, you will never perish, but I am talking about the blessings that the Lord lavishes on you from day to day. They are given in order that you may share them with others. To what extent do you share your blessings?

I would have you think of three things. First, to what extent do you use your *time* for the blessing of other people? When I find Christians who need so much physical recreation and have so little time to seek to win souls, I do not quite understand it. I was speaking with a young man some months ago, and I said, "Do you do anything to win others for Christ?" He said, "I would like to, but it doesn't seem to be my gift. I work hard all day, and when Saturday comes I have to go off and get some physical exercise." I think his great invigorating exercise was throwing horseshoes at a little stick. I said, "Did it ever strike you that you could get wonderful exercise by taking a bundle of tracts and going out on a country road and visiting the homes along the way, telling people about their souls?

Walking is wonderful exercise." "But," he said, "I am thinking of serious things all week, and I cannot be serious on Saturday afternoon."

Time is given us to use in view of eternity. I quite recognize that we need a certain amount of physical exercise or we would go to pieces, but you will find you can get on beautifully if you give more of your time to God. I was saved forty-one years ago, and I can honestly say that since that time my best days have been those in which I have spent my time trying to help other people gain a knowledge of Christ; it is the greatest exercise in the world.

I was visiting a preacher some time ago, and he asked, "What do you do for physical exercise?" I replied, "I preach." "But I mean when you want to get a rest," he said. "I preach some more and that rests me," I answered; "the more I do in the work of the Lord, the better I feel." "Brother," he said, "you will have a nervous breakdown if you are not careful." "But I am trying to be careful," I said. It isn't the Lord's work that gives people nervous breakdowns; it is getting into debt, getting mixed up in questionable things, and then getting worried and upset. Just keep at solid service for the Lord Jesus Christ, and you will not have a nervous breakdown.

Paul was in the Lord's service for thirty years. His enemies tried to kill him again and again; he was half-drowned several times, and was thrown to wild beasts. But the old man, when about seventy years of age, had much more vigor than a lot of worldly preachers that I meet who have to go on a prolonged vacation every once in a while. Your time belongs to the Lord Jesus, and He gives it to you in order that you may use it to bless and help others. "Look not every man on his own things, but every man also on the things of others" (Philippians 2:4).

Some time ago, I knew a dear man, one of the greatest men for physical exercise I ever saw. He worked hard on the street railroad. I would see him down on his knees, a great big covering over his eyes to shield them from the brilliant light, as he welded the steel rails. By Saturday noon, he was just worn out. He would get a bundle of books and off he would go for exercise, over the hills and far away, hunting up poor needy souls, maybe in the county hospital, possibly in the jails, and to poor families. Sometimes he would hear of somebody lying sick and poor and miserable, and he would go to see that one. He had a remarkable way of preaching the gospel. He would often lay down a five-dollar bill at the side of a sick person's bed, if he found out that the family had no money to pay the bills. On Sunday he would say, "My! I was worn out yesterday, but I had a wonderful time Saturday afternoon, and I am all rested up." He found his rest in living for others.

> Live for others while on earth you live,
> Give to others what you have to give.

Then you will find the secret of a really happy Christian life. Your time is to be spent in the service of Christ for the blessing of others, for the blessing of the "little sister," or that poor brother.

God has not only given you the blessing of time, He has entrusted you with your *talents.* "Oh, but," you say, "I haven't any." Oh yes, you have. You would not like it if others said you had no talents. But who are you using them for? For Christ, for the blessing of that brother, of that sister in need? It is the investment that you make of your talents here for the glory of the Lord Jesus Christ that is going to bring you a reward at His judgment seat. You remember that He said, "Unto every one that hath shall be given...but from him that hath not shall be taken away even that which he hath" (Matthew 25:29). You are to use the talents God has given you for Jesus' sake. Is it the ability to speak? Use it for winning souls to Christ. Is it that you know how to be a kindly sympathetic friend? Then surely you have a wonderful sphere for service. Is it looking up the shut-ins, the sick and needy, and giving them a tender loving word? You would bless and help so many you never think of now, if you would only begin to use those talents for Him. Christian service is not just the work of the man on the platform. Whenever I see souls coming to Christ in a meeting, I wonder what started them.

Years ago, when I was young and ignorant, I would go home to my wife and say, "I won six souls tonight." She would look at me and say, "Are you sure you did it?" I would say, "No," of course, "but the Lord used me." But you know it really began long before that. Perhaps it was a dear Sunday school teacher who had been sowing the seed in the heart of that young man or woman. It was lying there dormant for days, months, or years; as the Word of God came anew, something was said that just caused it to fructify and burst into life, and that boy or girl came to Jesus. Perhaps it was the lesson the mother taught as the child sat on her lap long ago. Perhaps it was the father's word dropped into the heart. There is seldom a soul who comes to Christ without many people having a part in it. It is not just the preacher and the preached message. God gives us our talents to be used for Christ. Paul planted, Apollos watered, "but God gave the increase" (1 Corinthians 3:6).

Then there is my privilege not only to use my time and my talents but my *money* to help and bless that little sister, that neglected brother. What a wonderful thing consecrated money is! There never would have been a dollar bill, a piece of silver money, a gold, copper, or nickel coin in the world, if it had not been for sin. That is why Jesus called it the mammon of unrighteousness. Every coin in your pocket is a witness that sin has come into the world. If men and women had remained as they were when God created them, there would have been no money. People would not have sought to build up fortunes and buy and sell things. We would still be living in a glorious state on this earth, and we would not have had to go out and earn our bread by the sweat of our brow.

However, Jesus said, "Make to yourselves friends of the mammon of unrighteousness; that, when ye fail, they may receive you into everlasting habitations" (Luke 16:9). Since money is here, and we cannot get along without it, do not live for it; do not let it get a hold on you—"The love of money is the root of all evil" (1 Timothy 6:10). Use it now with an eye on your everlasting home. Use it to meet, of course, your own needs and those of your family; but then use it as God enables you, to bless and help others in their deep spiritual need and in their temporal need too. Then, when at last you reach the glorious habitation, you will see a throng running down the golden street to meet you. They will say, "Welcome," and you will ask in amazement, "Who can these be?" And one will answer,

"We are so glad to welcome you here, for it was your dollar that paid for that Testament that brought me the message of Christ." Another, "You met my need when in such distress I thought nobody cared for me. You gave me the money for a good dinner, and I could not help but think of the God of all grace who had put it in your heart to do that for me." And another may say, "I came to Jesus because of the kind deed you did for me." Then we will feel it was worthwhile that we spent and were spent for others. "What shall be done for our little sister?" Let us share with her the good things we have.

The king in Song of Solomon said, "If she be a wall, we will build upon her a palace of silver" (9). A wall speaks of security. If she has already entered into the blessings and security of Christ, we will help her and build her up in the things of Christ. We will add to that which is already hers. "If she be a door, we will inclose her with boards of cedar" (9). A door speaks of responsibility, or opportunity for service. "A great door," said the apostle, "and effectual is opened unto me, and there are many adversaries" (1 Corinthians 16:9). "Behold, I have set before thee an open door, and no man can shut it: for thou hast a little strength, and hast kept my word, and hast not denied my name" (Revelation 3:8). But what use is a door if it has no side-posts to swing from? "If she be a door, we will inclose her with boards of cedar." If she wants an opportunity for service, we will help to make it possible. We will assist her in whatever is required, that she may work the better for the Lord Jesus Christ.

Then as the chapter and the little book close, the bride, her heart content to think she and her little sister too have come into blessing, goes over the past. She talks about the vineyard days, the love that has been shown and the bliss now hers. Then she turns to her beloved one and says, "Make haste, my beloved, and be thou like to a roe or to a young hart upon the mountains of spices" (14). "Until the day break, and the shadows flee away" (2:17). The consummation of all bliss will be when we are at home forever with Him. Until then, let us seek to spend and be spent for His glory.

Once a missionary offering was being taken and as the box was handed to a very wealthy man, he brushed it to one side and said, "I do not believe in missions." "Then," said the usher, "take something out; this is for the heathen." How can you be a real Christian and not be concerned about those who are less privileged than you are? May God stir our hearts to think of the millions that are still in great, great need. If we can do nothing else for them, we can bring their case to Him; we can be prayer-helpers; we can intercede on their behalf. The wonderful thing is that when you begin to pray, the rest follows. People who pray devise ways and means for giving.

A lady said to me one time, "You know my husband is unsaved, and he never lets me have any money. He says he wouldn't for the world give me a dime to put in the missionary offering. But I started praying about missions, and as I prayed, there came such a burden on my heart to do something. I had two or three chickens that I had bought with a little money I received from doing some sewing for a neighbor. The money from the chickens was all mine, and I said, 'I am going to devote one chicken to the Lord, and every egg that this chicken lays will belong to Him.' It has been wonderful to me to see that the other chickens lay every once in a while, but my husband growls and says, 'That missionary chicken of yours lays nearly two eggs a day.' Of course that is an exaggeration, but every little while I have another dozen eggs, and I take them to the corner store and get my money, and that goes for missions."

I believe that the Lord will take that money and do with it what He did with the five loaves and two fishes: multiply, and multiply, and multiply it. Maybe one way in which He will multiply this lady's gift will be to start some of you giving. Then the Lord will turn to this lady and say, "You are the woman that had that chicken the preacher told about. I am going to give you a part of the reward, for these folk just followed your example!"

Let us seek by grace to make every day count for the blessing of others. If we truly love Him we cannot be selfish or indifferent to the needs of those for whom He died, "until the day break, and the shadows flee away."

AUTHOR BIOGRAPHY

HENRY ALLAN IRONSIDE, one of the twentieth century's greatest preachers, was born in Toronto, Canada, on October 14, 1876. He lived his life by faith; his needs at crucial moments were met in the most remarkable ways.

Though his classes stopped with grammar school, his fondness for reading and an incredibly retentive memory put learning to use. His scholarship was well recognized in academic circles with Wheaton College awarding an honorary Litt.D. in 1930 and Bob Jones University an honorary D.D. in 1942. Dr. Ironside was also appointed to the boards of numerous Bible institutes, seminaries, and Christian organizations.

"HAI" lived to preach and he did so widely throughout the United States and abroad. E. Schuyler English, in his biography of Ironside, revealed that during 1948, the year HAI was 72, and in spite of failing eyesight, he "gave 569 addresses, besides participating in many other ways." In his eighteen years at Chicago's Moody Memorial Church, his only pastorate, every Sunday but two had at least one profession of faith in Christ.

H. A. Ironside went to be with the Lord on January 15, 1951. Throughout his ministry, he authored expositions on 51 books of the Bible and through the great clarity of his messages led hundreds of thousands, worldwide, to a knowledge of God's Word. His words are as fresh and meaningful today as when first preached.

The official biography of Dr. Ironside, *H. A. Ironside: Ordained of the Lord*, is available from the publisher.

THE WRITTEN MINISTRY OF
H. A. IRONSIDE

Expositions

Joshua
Ezra
Nehemiah
Esther
Psalms (1-41 only)
Proverbs
Song of Solomon
Isaiah
Jeremiah
Lamentations
Ezekiel
Daniel
The Minor Prophets
Matthew
Mark
Luke
John

Acts
Romans
1 & 2 Corinthians
Galatians
Ephesians
Philippians
Colossians
1 & 2 Thessalonians
1 & 2 Timothy
Titus
Philemon
Hebrews
James
1 & 2 Peter
1,2, & 3 John
Jude
Revelation

Doctrinal Works

Baptism
Death and Afterward
Eternal Security of the Believer
Holiness: The False and
    the True
The Holy Trinity

Letters to a Roman Catholic
    Priest
The Levitical Offerings
Not Wrath But Rapture
Wrongly Dividing the Word
    of Truth

Historical Works

The Four Hundred Silent Years
A Historical Sketch of the Brethren Movement

Other works by the author are brought back into print from time to time.
All of this material is available from your local Christian bookstore or from
the publisher.

LOIZEAUX

A Heritage of Ministry . . .

Paul and Timothy Loizeaux began their printing and publishing activities in the farming community of Vinton, Iowa, in 1876. Their tools were rudimentary: a hand press, several fonts of loose type, ink, and a small supply of paper. There was certainly no dream of a thriving commercial enterprise. It was merely the means of supplying the literature needs for their own ministries, with the hope that the Lord would grant a wider circulation. It wasn't a business; it was a ministry.

Our Foundation Is the Word of God

We stand without embarrassment on the great fundamentals of the faith: the inspiration and authority of Scripture, the deity and spotless humanity of our Lord Jesus Christ, His atoning sacrifice and resurrection, the indwelling of the Holy Spirit, the unity of the church, the second coming of the Lord, and the eternal destinies of the saved and lost.

Our Mission Is to Help People Understand God's Word

We are not in the entertainment business. We only publish books and computer software we believe will be of genuine help to God's people, both through the faithful exposition of Scripture and practical application of its principles to contemporary need.

Faithfulness to the Word and consistency in what we publish have been hallmarks of Loizeaux through four generations. And that means when you see the name Loizeaux on the outside, you can trust what is on the inside. That is our promise to the Lord...and to you.

If Paul and Timothy were to visit us today they would still recognize the work they began in 1876. Because some very important things haven't changed at all...this is still a ministry.